TRADEMARKS AND SYMBOLS OF THE WORLD

TRADEMARKS AND SYMBOLS OF THE WORLD

BY
YUSAKU KAMEKURA
PREFACE BY
PAUL RAND

REINHOLD PUBLISHING CORPORATION
New York

CONTENTS

Published in the United States of America
by Reinhold Publishing Corporation, New York, 1965
Printed and bound in Japan
by Zokeisha Publications Limited, Tokyo

Library of Congress Catalog Card No. 65-24055

PREFACE

A few years ago, in an introduction to a collection of my own trademarks, I wrote the following:

A trademark
is a picture.
It is a symbol
a sign
an emblem
an escutcheon
...an image.

There are
good symbols...
like the cross.
There are
others...
like the swastika.
Their meanings
are taken
from reality.

Symbols
are a duality.
They take on
meaning

from causes
...good or bad.
And they give
meaning
to causes
...good or bad.
The flag
is a symbol
of a country.
The cross
is a symbol
of a religion.
The swastika
was a symbol
of good luck
until
its meaning
was changed.

The vitality
of a symbol
comes
from effective
dissemination...
by the state
by the community
by the church
by the corporation.
It needs
attending
to get
attention.

The trademark
is a symbol
of a corporation.
It is not
a sign of
quality...
it is a sign of
the quality.
The trademark
for Chanel
smells
as good as
the perfume
it stands for.
This
is the blending
of form
and content.

Trademarks
are animate
inanimate
organic
geometric.
They are letters
ideograms
monograms
colors
things.
Ideally
they do not
illustrate
they indicate.
They are not
representational
but suggestive.

A trademark
is created
by a designer,
but *made*
by a corporation.
A trademark
is a picture,
an image...
the image
of a corporation.

In assembling his first book, *Trademarks of the World*, Mr. Kamekura focused our attention on the universality of the problem of identification and, happily, on the high level of imagination and skill that designers of many countries have brought to bear on this most important and difficult design assignment.

In this new book he goes one step further, showing us not only the trademarks but, more importantly, their application to a variety of practical problems. Not only do we gain insight into the designer's skills around the world; but, from Kamekura's selections for this volume, we learn something of the taste and viewpoint of a singular designer.

Weston, Connecticut 1965

Paul Rand

FOREWORD

When I wrote my previous book *Trademarks of the World* (New York, 1956), Bernard Rudofsky chided me by saying, "You must not bring out such a convenient book. It will only spoil designers by making it too easy for them." These words, coming from a man whose work I greatly admire, gave me much food for thought. Nevertheless, ten years later, I have prepared another "convenient" book.

After the previous work had gone through several printings, and I was on the point of letting it die a natural death, I received numerous requests for a revised edition incorporating additional material. After long deliberation, I finally decided that it would be better to prepare an entirely new book of the outstanding trademarks and symbols created during the last ten years. I was fortunate in receiving the greatest cooperation from outstanding designers throughout the world, who generously sent me samples of their work. I take this opportunity to thank them for their assistance which has made this book possible.

The reader who looks at this book, will not find anything "Japanese" about it, even though the author is a Japanese. However, I am firmly of the opinion that trademarks, symbols, and signs must speak an international language.

This book contains 763 entries selected from about 2,000 items received. I have tried to express my own attitudes in the way the entries are arranged, and in the rhythm that this has created.

I have no intention of providing a long text. I hope that the selection and arrangement of the items included, and the rhythm they carry, are themselves a visual essay in an international language.

As he did for my previous book, Paul Rand was good enough to contribute a splendid preface, for which I am deeply grateful. I am indeed proud to be able to call this great artist my friend.

I would also like to thank Miss Yumiko Onishi for her assistance throughout the entire lengthy process of compiling this book.

Tokyo, April 1965

Yusaku Kamekura

2

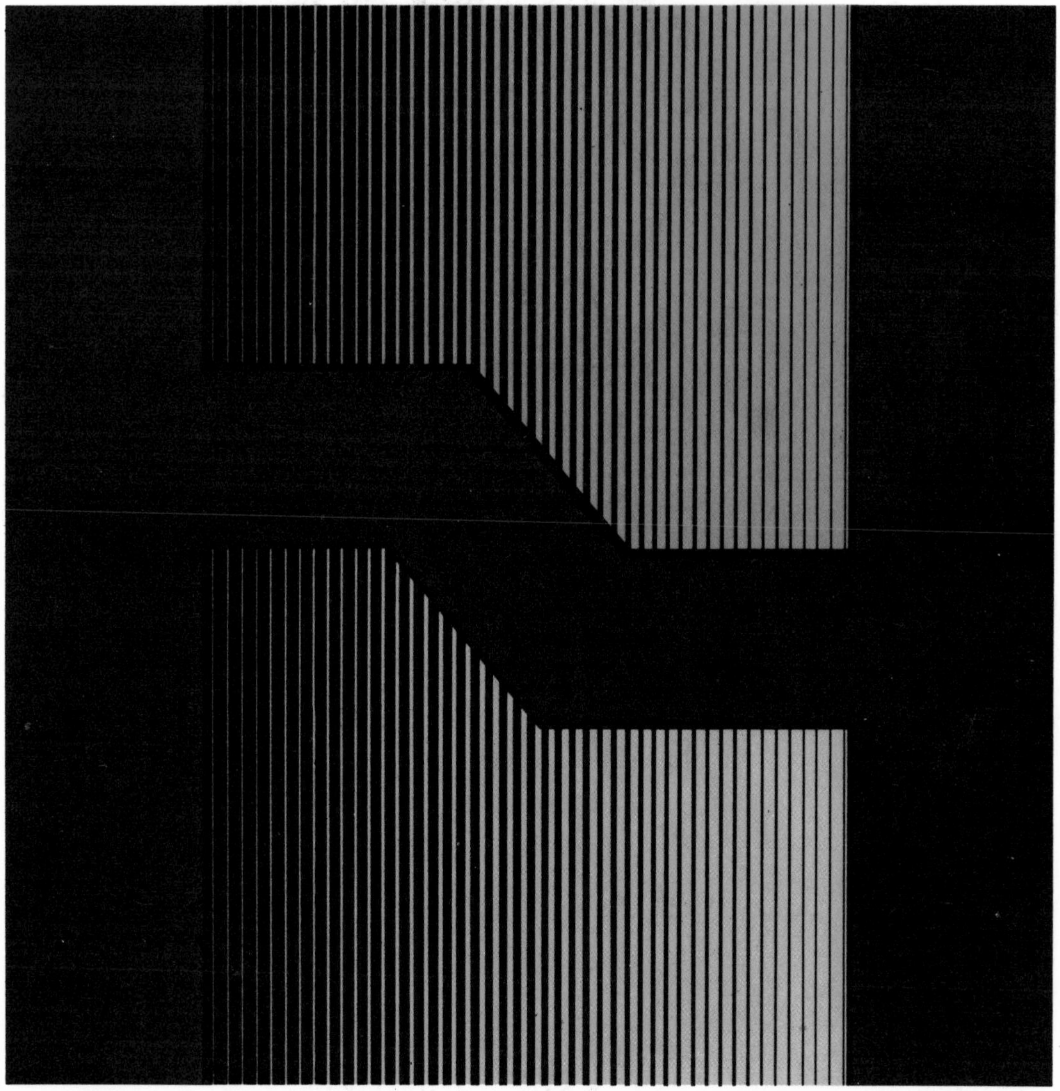

3

4

5

FULLER
PAINTS

6

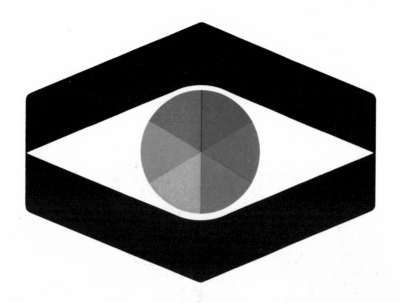

7

8

9

10

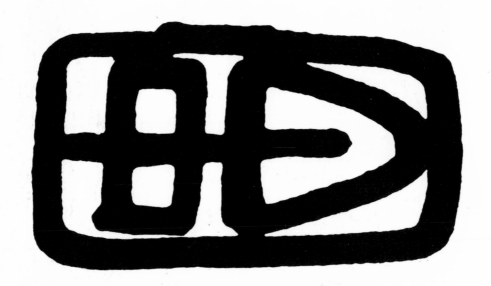

LIGHTCRAFT
11

12

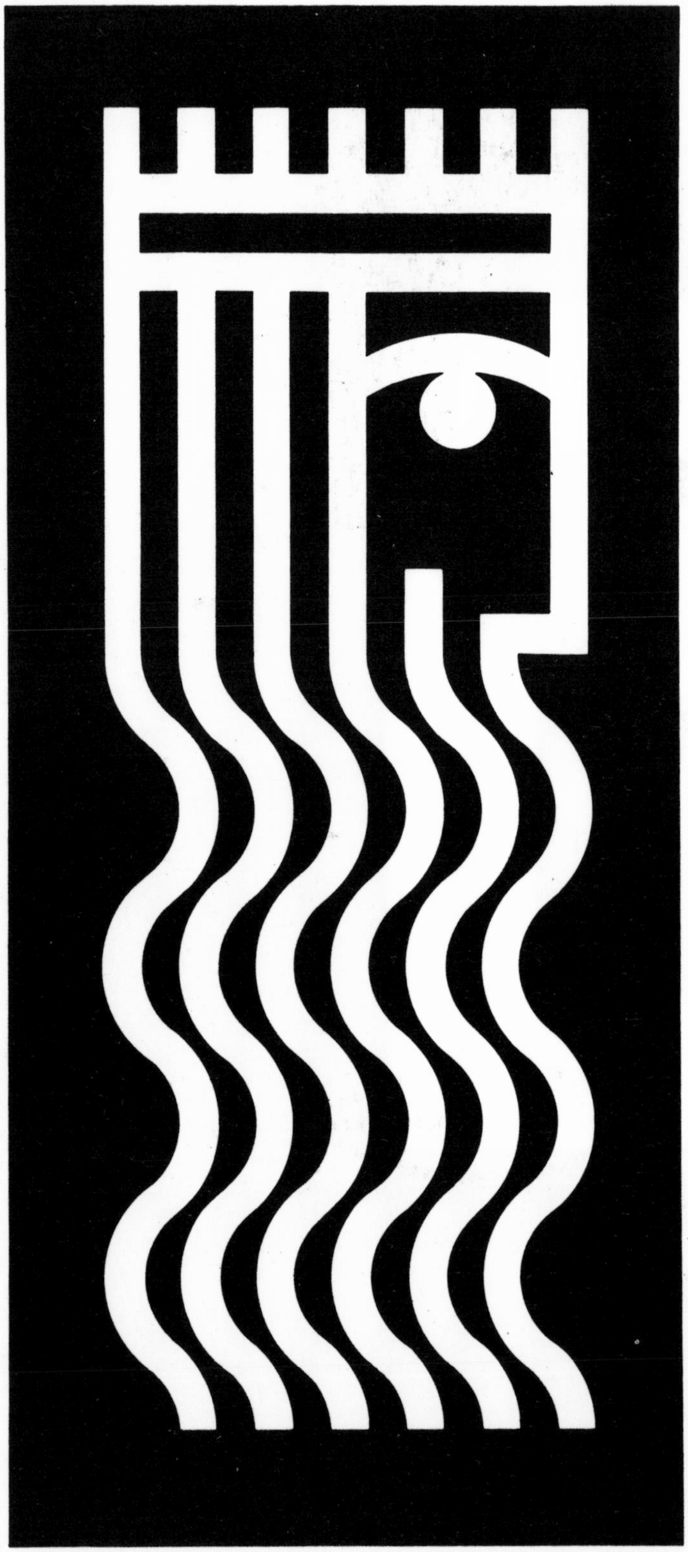

13

14

15

IBM
Typewriter Ribbons
IBM
IBM
IBM
IBM
One half gross
Mechanical Mark Sensing
Electrographic Pencils
"Selectric"
Ribbon
Cartridge
IBM
IBM
Executary Microphone
IBM
Ribbon
IBM
Ribbon

IBM

IBM

16

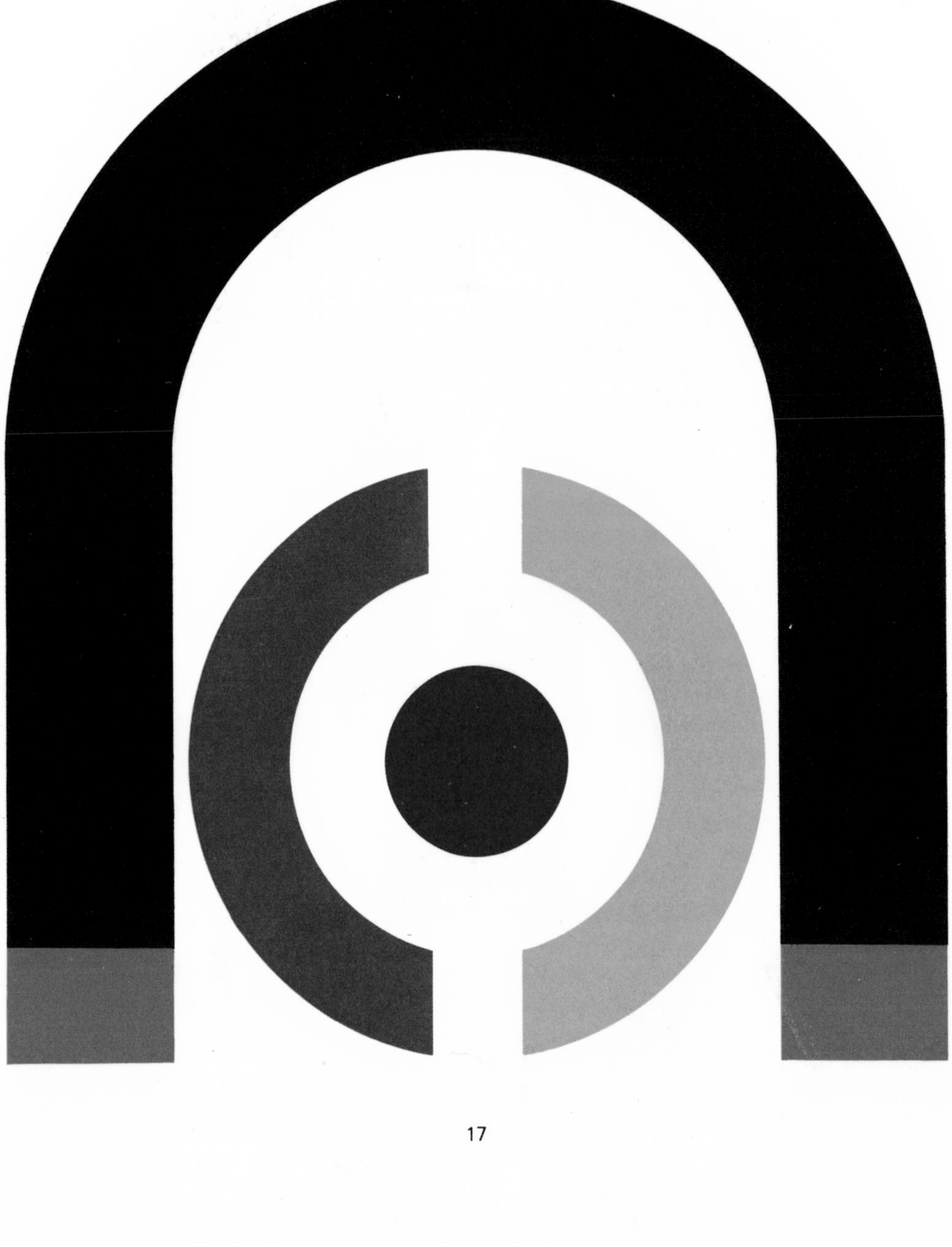

17

ania

Esclusività Maestrelli

18

19

ALBITEX

21

22

20

23

24

25

26

27

28

29

30

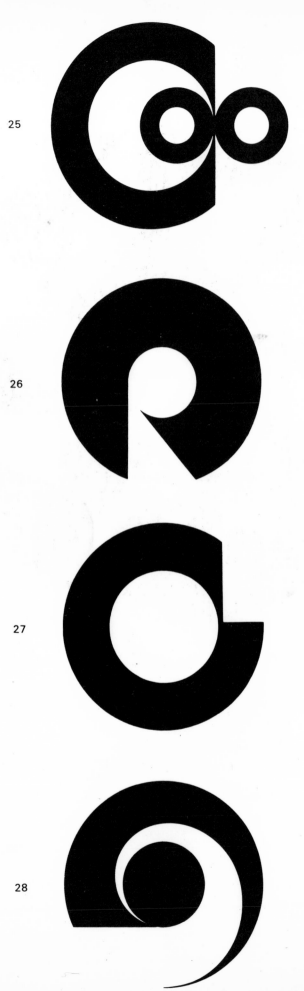

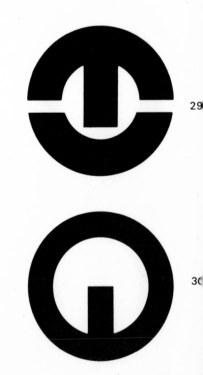

31

32

33

34

35

36

37

38

39

40

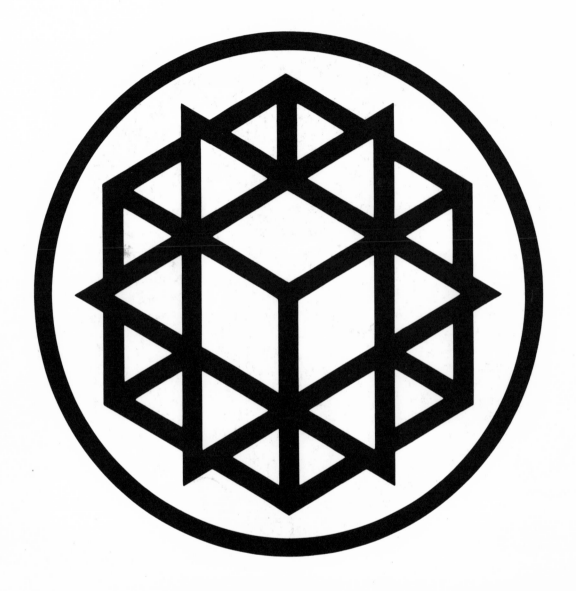

41

42

43

45

46

44

47

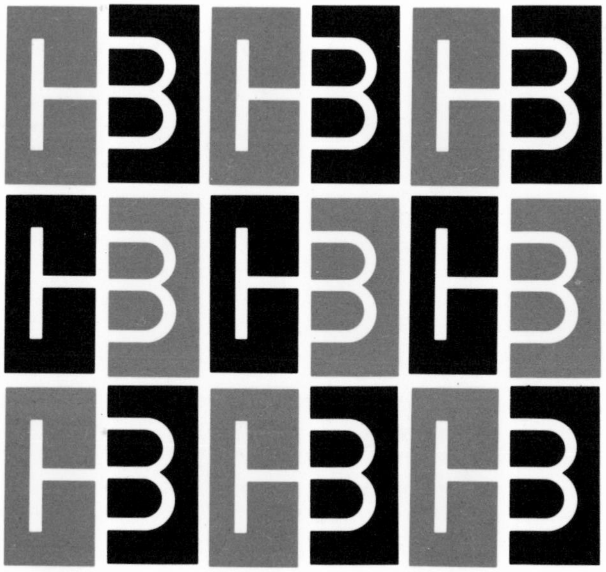

48

49

50

51

52

53

54

55

56

LIGNOPLAST

57

gromalto

58

59

60

61

62

63

ATLAS

64

65

66

67

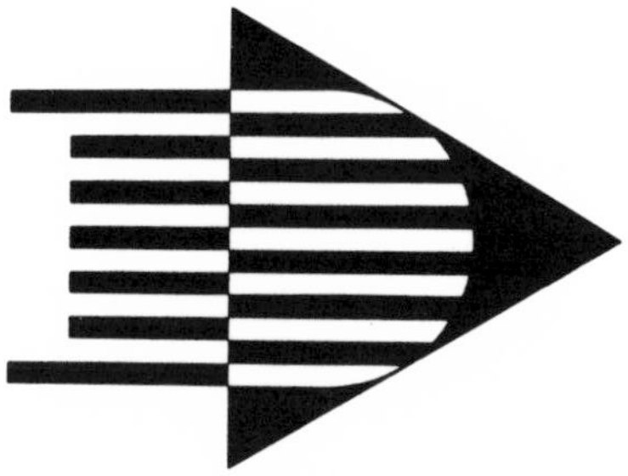

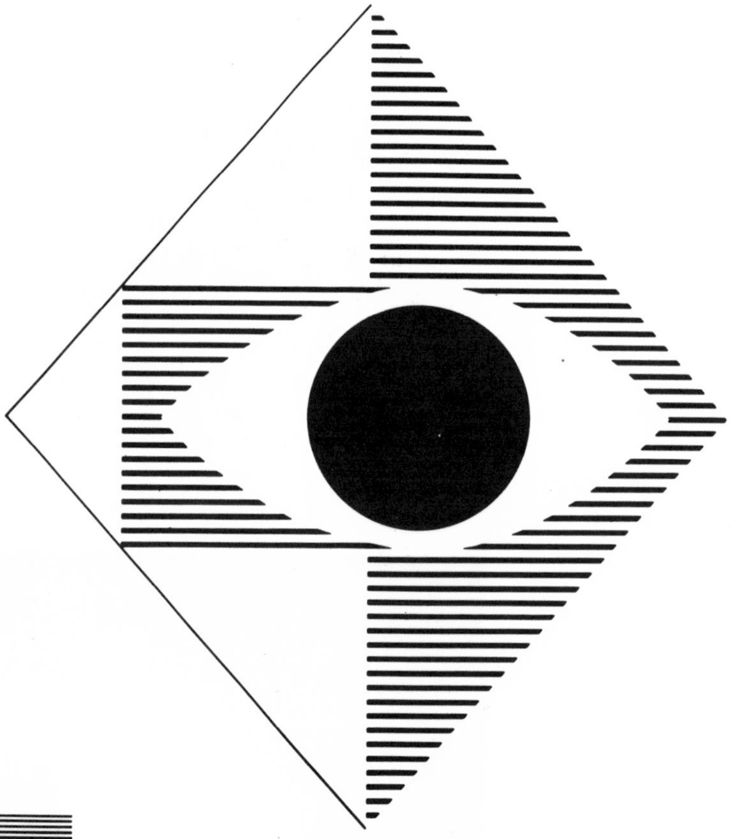

69

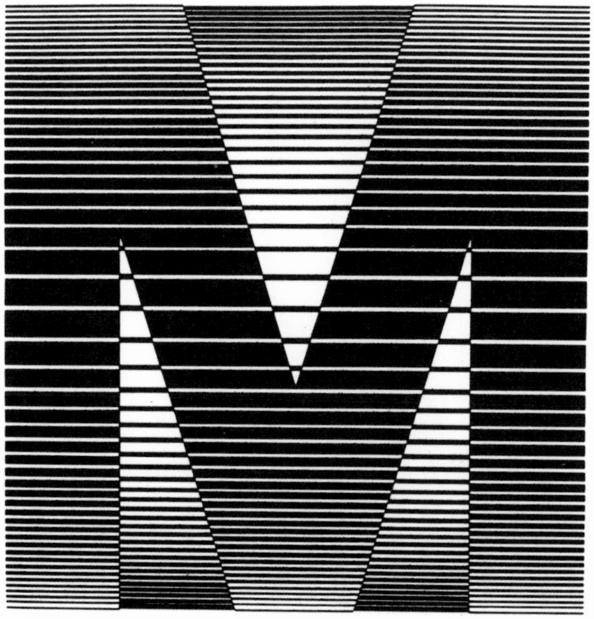

68

70

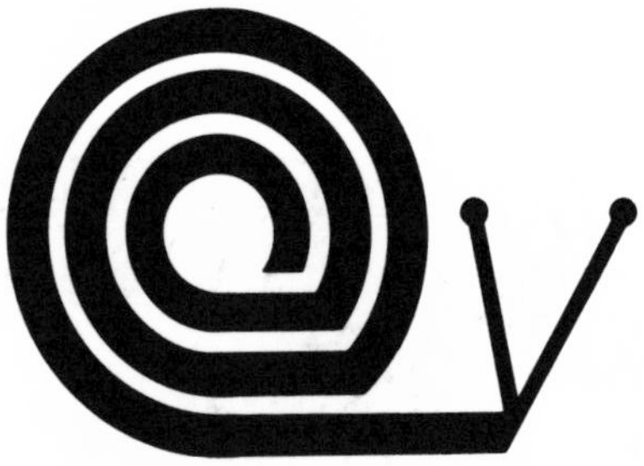

71

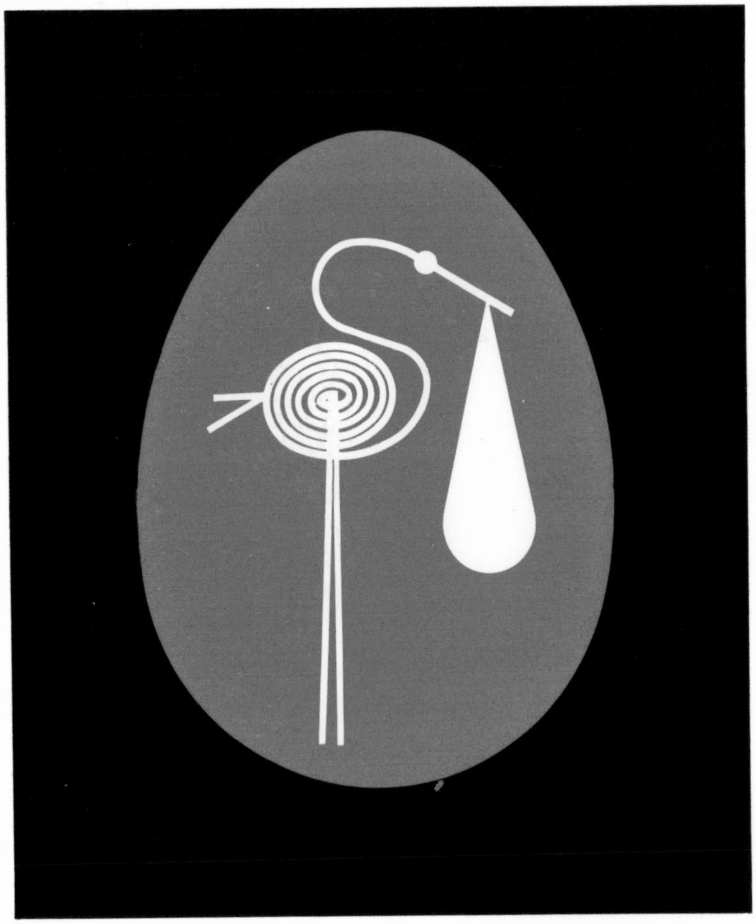

72

73

74

75

76

78

77

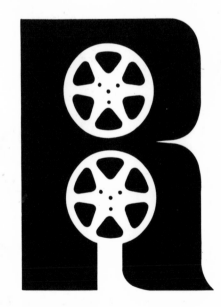

81

79

80

82

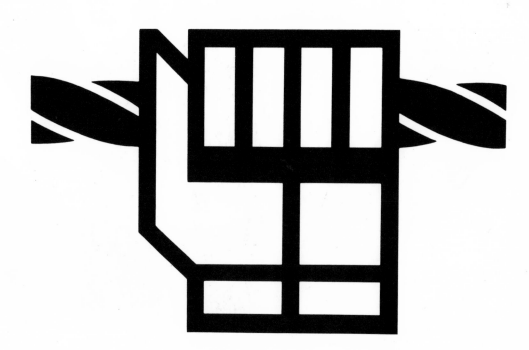

83

84

85

87

86

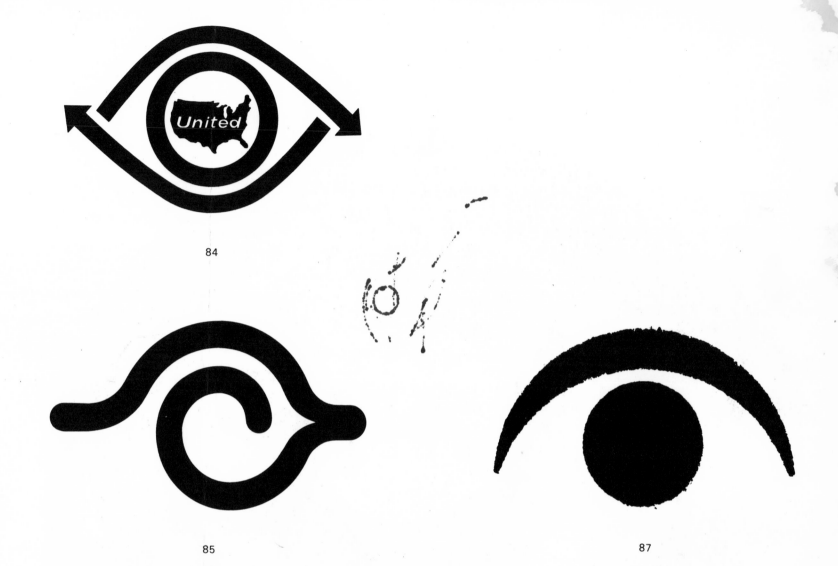

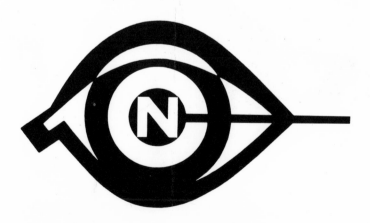

89

88

90

91

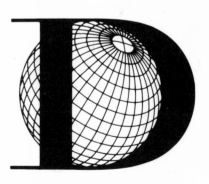

FILM

92

93

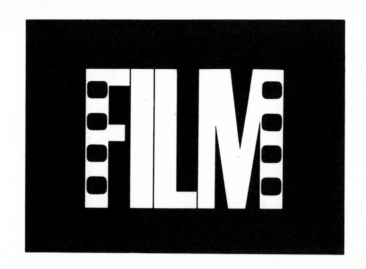

94

95

Libra

97

98

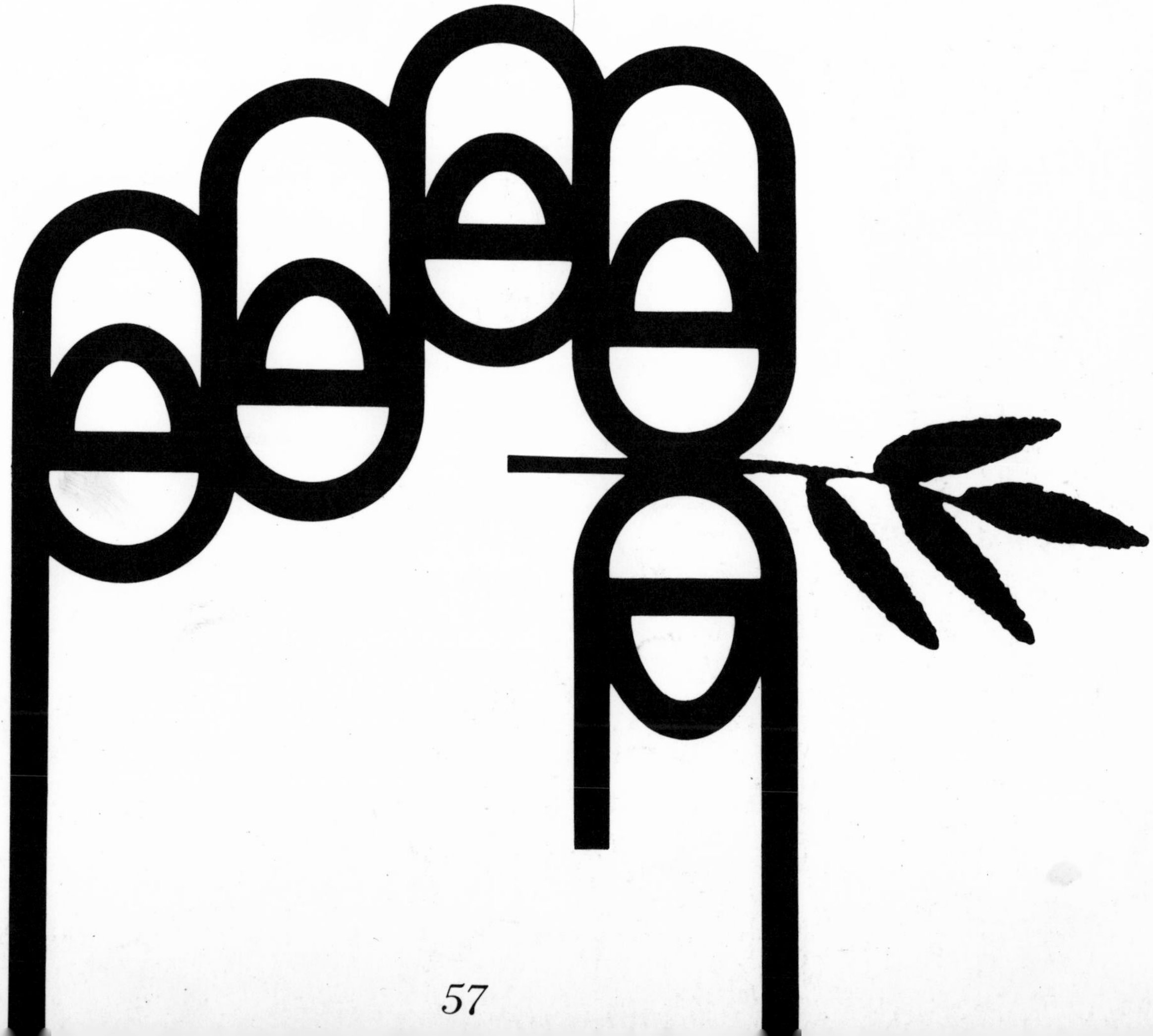

99

100

101

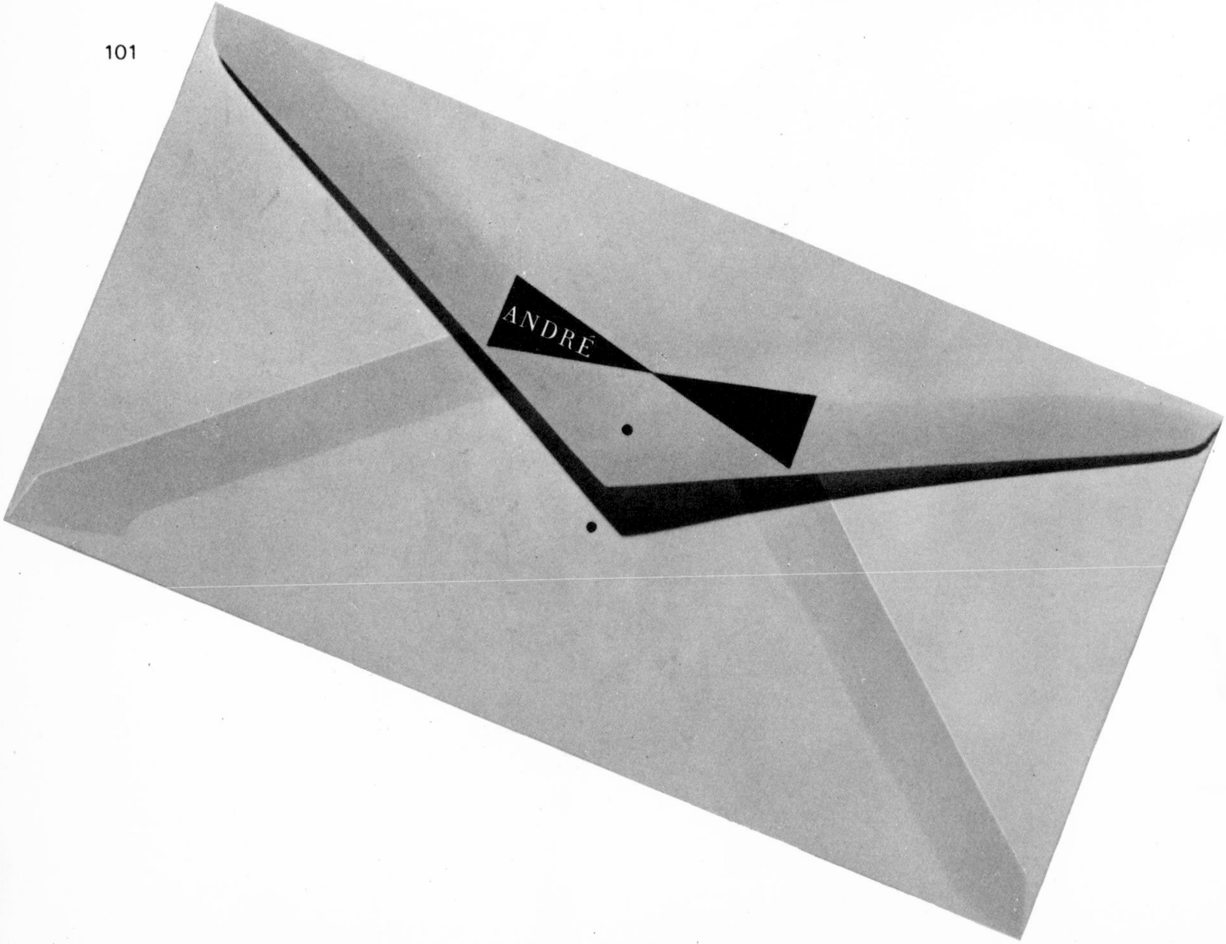

102

103

THE
TURKS
HEAD

104

105

106

107

108

Sand Grenade

109

110

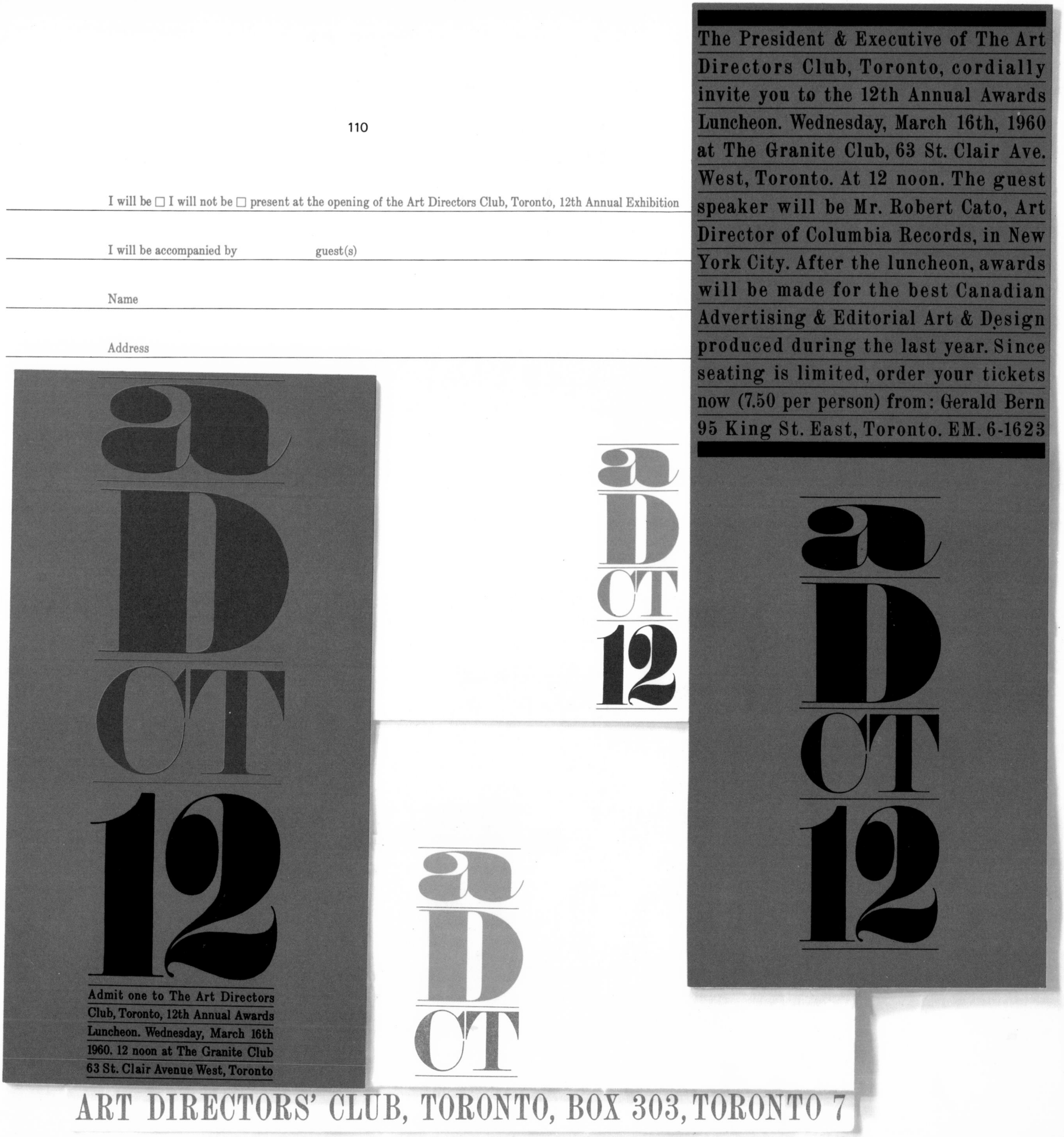
I will be ☐ I will not be ☐ present at the opening of the Art Directors Club, Toronto, 12th Annual Exhibition
I will be accompanied by guest(s)
Name
Address
aDCT12
Admit one to The Art Directors Club, Toronto, 12th Annual Awards Luncheon. Wednesday, March 16th 1960. 12 noon at The Granite Club 63 St. Clair Avenue West, Toronto
aDCT12
aDCT
ART DIRECTORS' CLUB, TORONTO, BOX 303, TORONTO 7
The President & Executive of The Art Directors Club, Toronto, cordially invite you to the 12th Annual Awards Luncheon. Wednesday, March 16th, 1960 at The Granite Club, 63 St. Clair Ave. West, Toronto. At 12 noon. The guest speaker will be Mr. Robert Cato, Art Director of Columbia Records, in New York City. After the luncheon, awards will be made for the best Canadian Advertising & Editorial Art & Design produced during the last year. Since seating is limited, order your tickets now (7.50 per person) from: Gerald Bern 95 King St. East, Toronto. EM. 6-1623
aDCT12

wohnbedarf

111

STEINER

112

113

Westab

114

alluminio

115

riri

116

therma

117

arflex

118

119

120

121

122

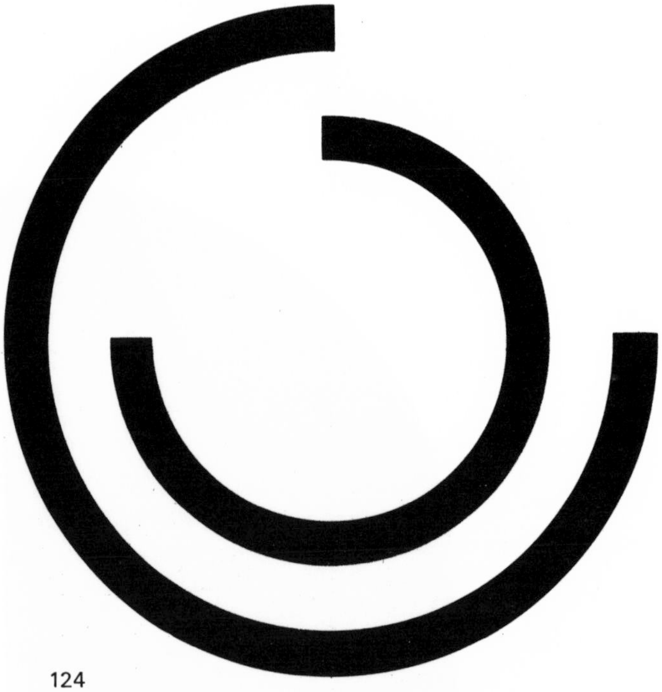

124

123

125

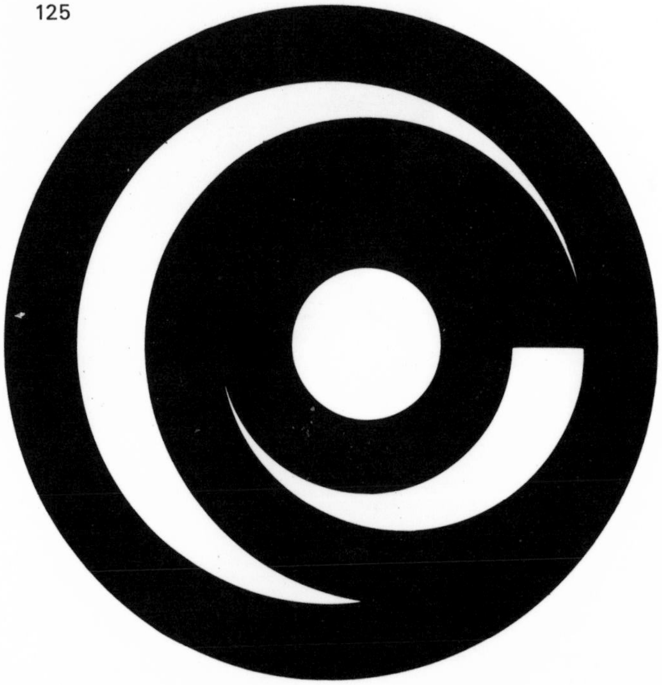

126
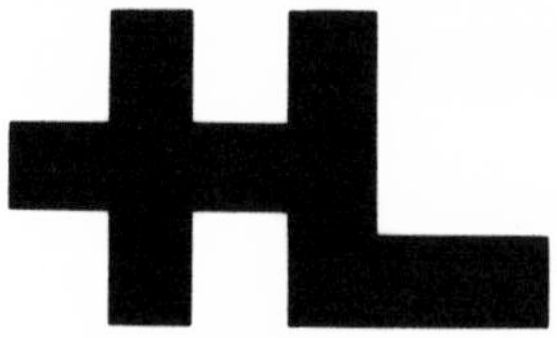

127
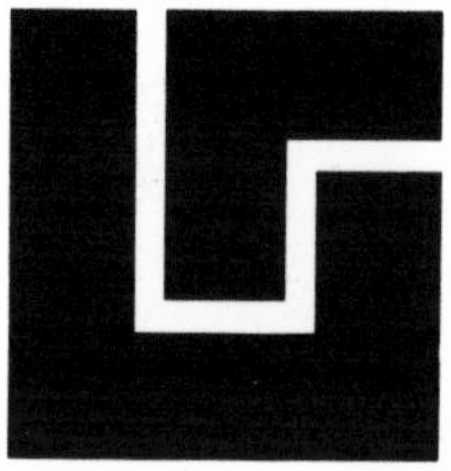

128
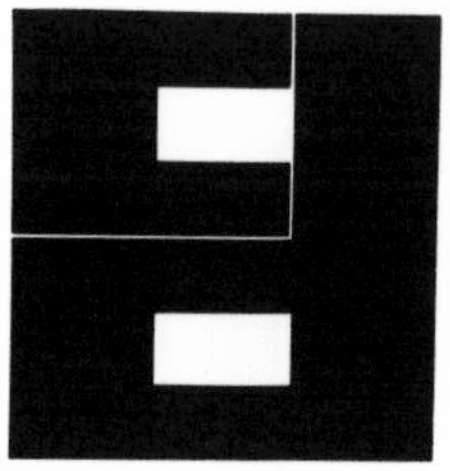

129

130
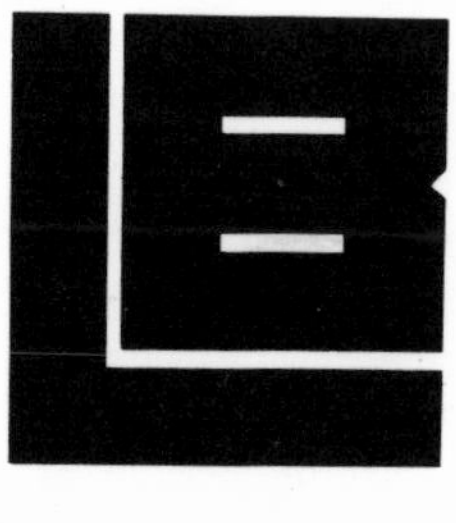

131
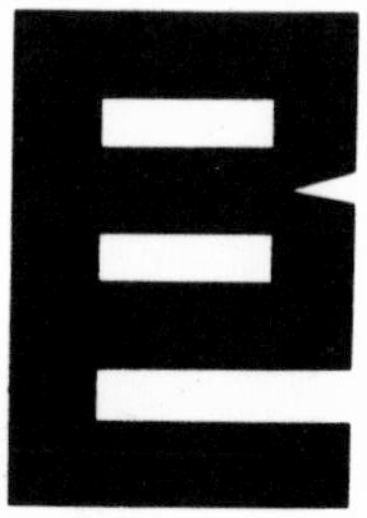

132
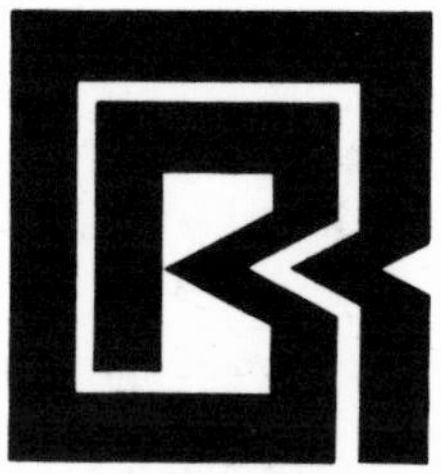

133
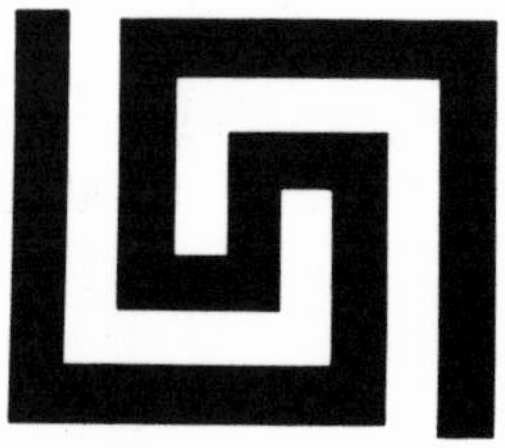

134
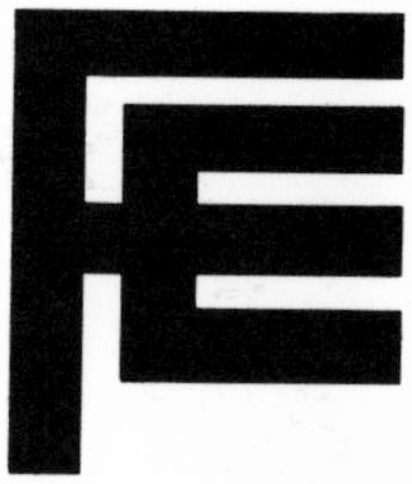

135
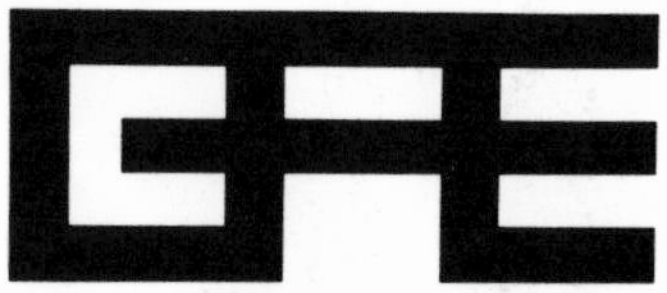

136
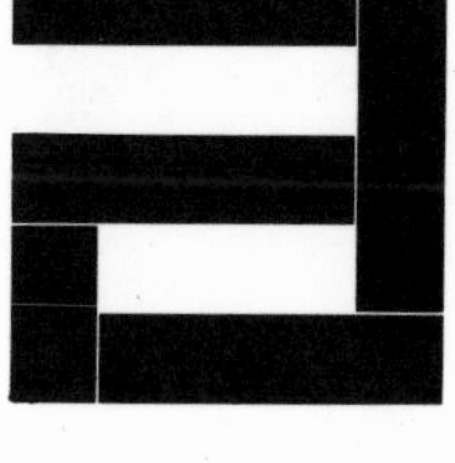

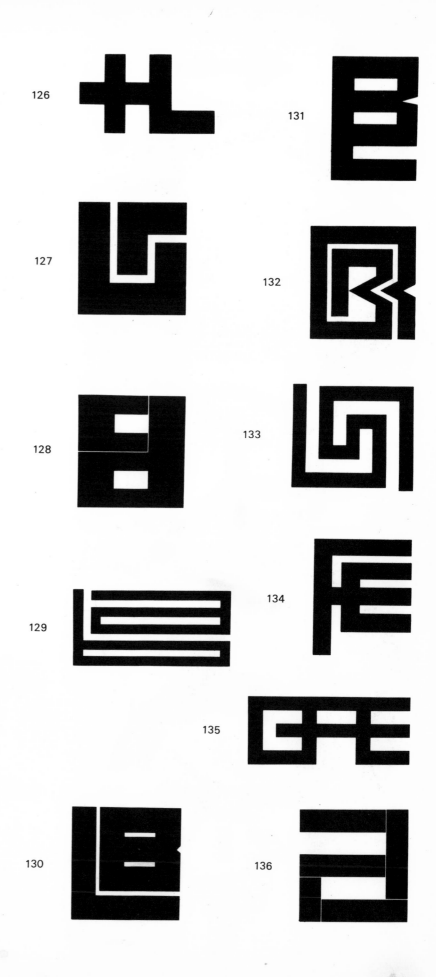

137

138

140

139

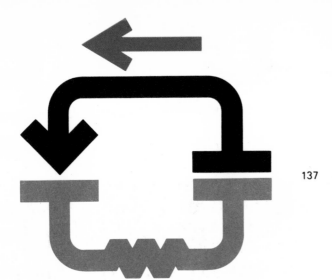

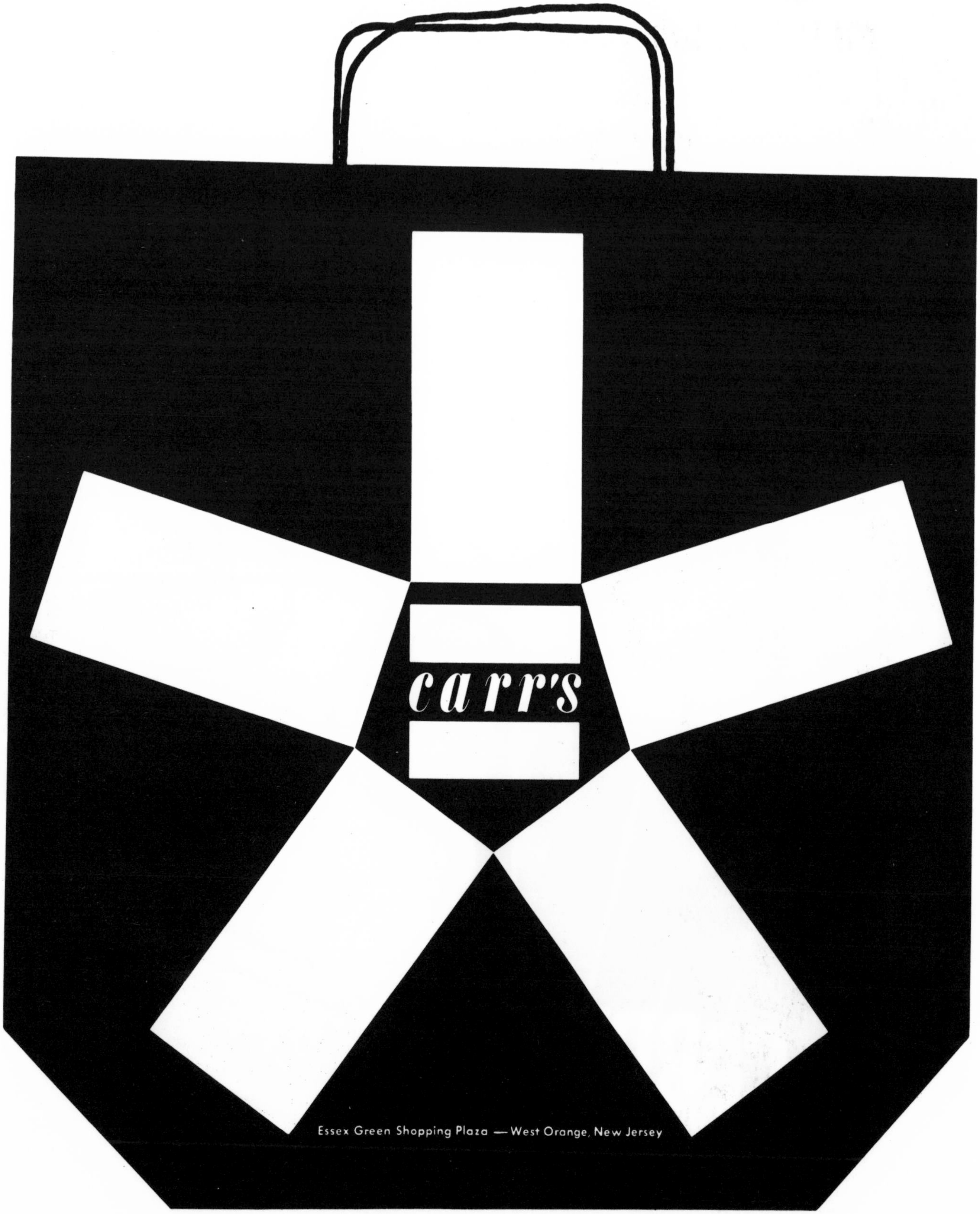
carr's
Essex Green Shopping Plaza — West Orange, New Jersey

142

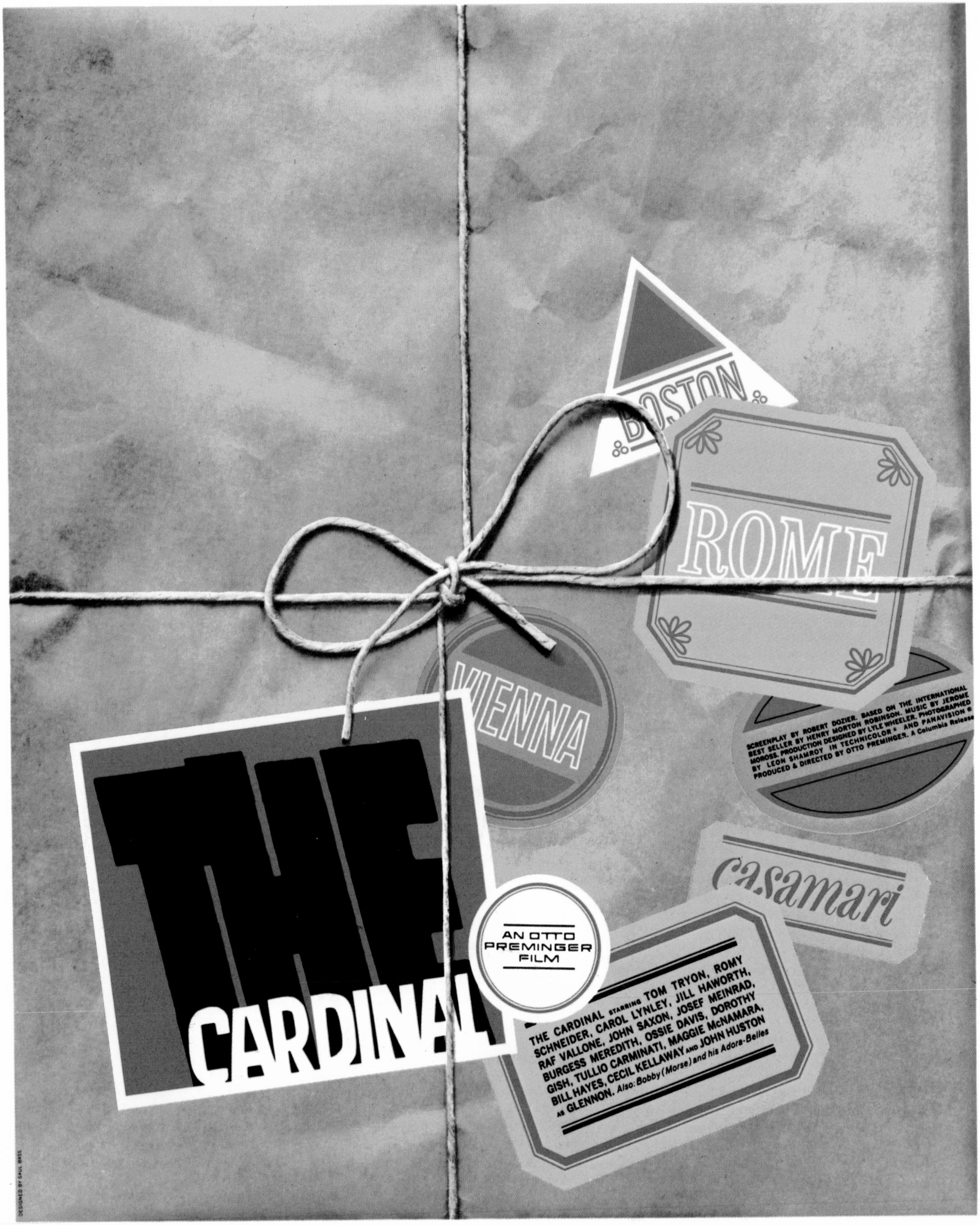
BOSTON
ROME
VIENNA
SCREENPLAY BY ROBERT DOZIER. BASED ON THE INTERNATIONAL BEST SELLER BY HENRY MORTON ROBINSON. MUSIC BY JEROME MOROSS. PRODUCTION DESIGNED BY LYLE WHEELER. PHOTOGRAPHED BY LEON SHAMROY IN TECHNICOLOR® AND PANAVISION® PRODUCED & DIRECTED BY OTTO PREMINGER. A Columbia Release
casamari
THE CARDINAL
AN OTTO PREMINGER FILM
THE CARDINAL STARRING TOM TRYON, ROMY SCHNEIDER, CAROL LYNLEY, JILL HAWORTH, RAF VALLONE, JOHN SAXON, JOSEF MEINRAD, BURGESS MEREDITH, OSSIE DAVIS, DOROTHY GISH, TULLIO CARMINATI, MAGGIE McNAMARA, BILL HAYES, CECIL KELLAWAY AND JOHN HUSTON AS GLENNON. Also: Bobby (Morse) and his Adora-Belles
DESIGNED BY SAUL BASS

143

144

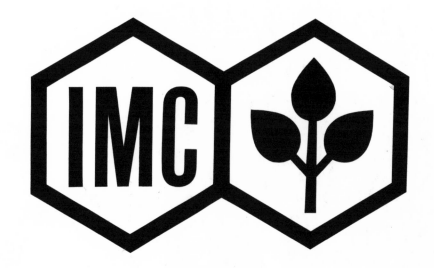

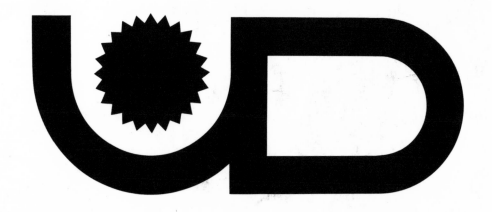

145

146

MT

147

pagina

148

HOCKEY

149

150

151

152

153

spinner.

155

154

157 MONO

156

158 miwa

159

160

161

162

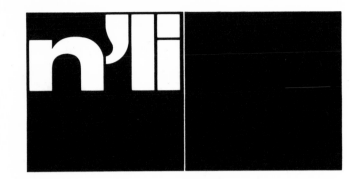

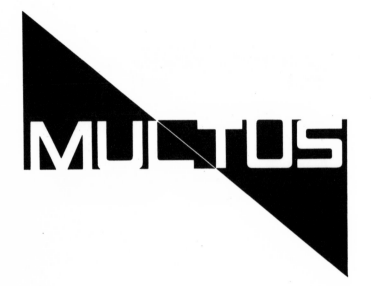

163

164

165

166

167

168

169

170

171

172

173

174

175

176

177

178

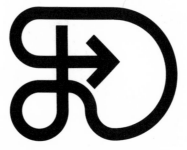

179

180

181

182

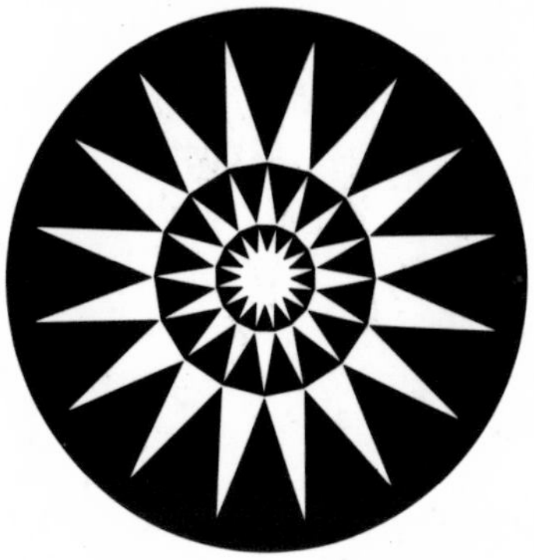

183

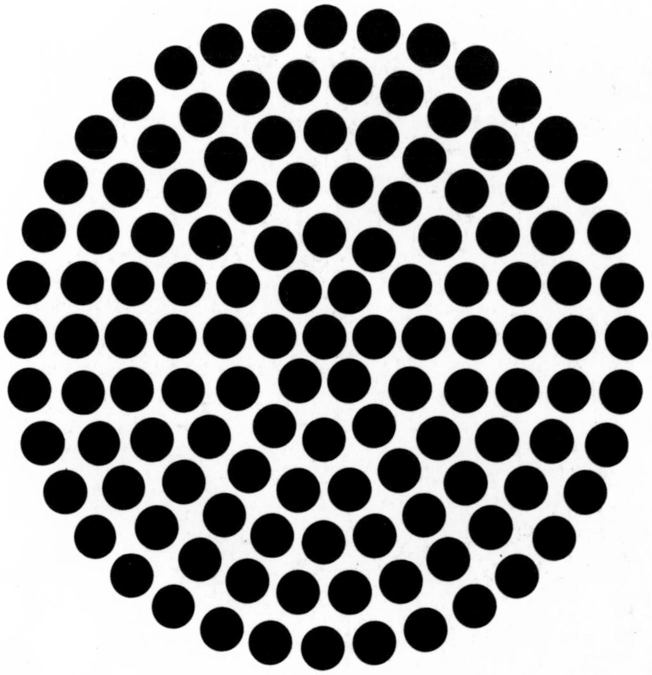

184

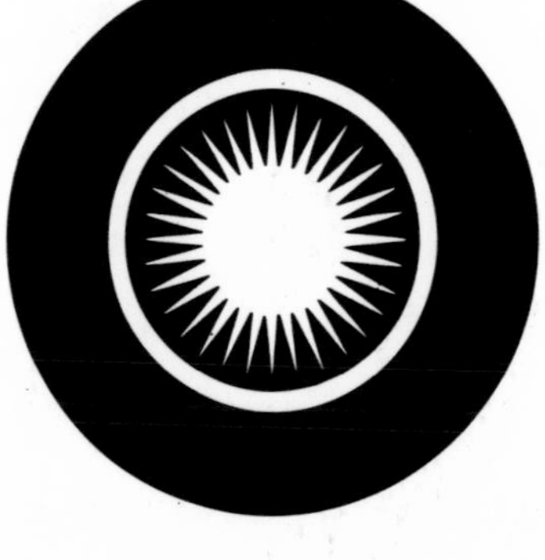

185

186

187 188

189 190

191 192

193 194

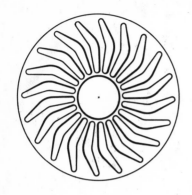

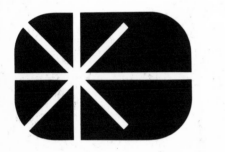

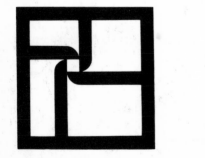

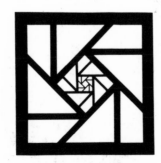

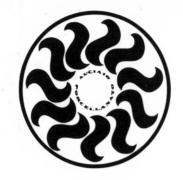

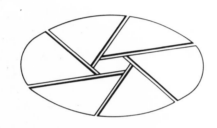

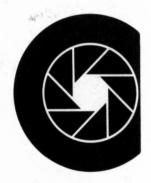

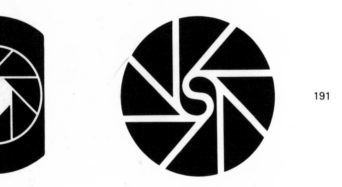

195

196

197

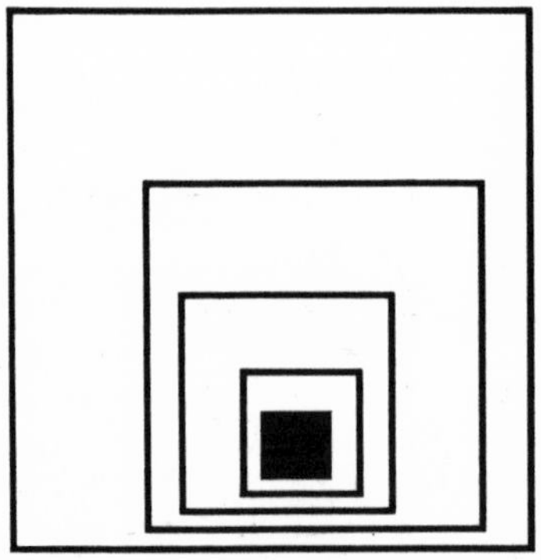

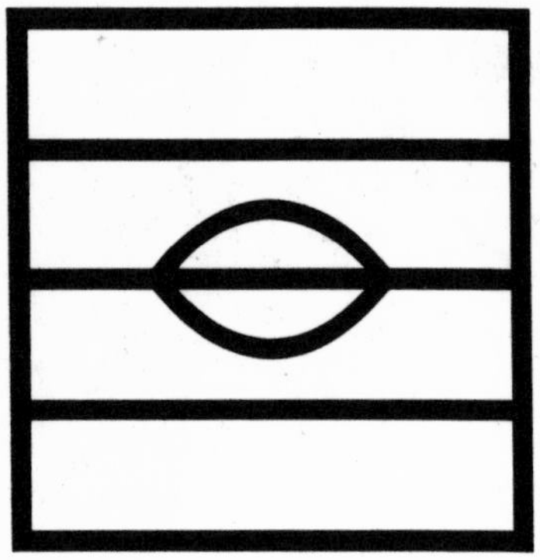

198

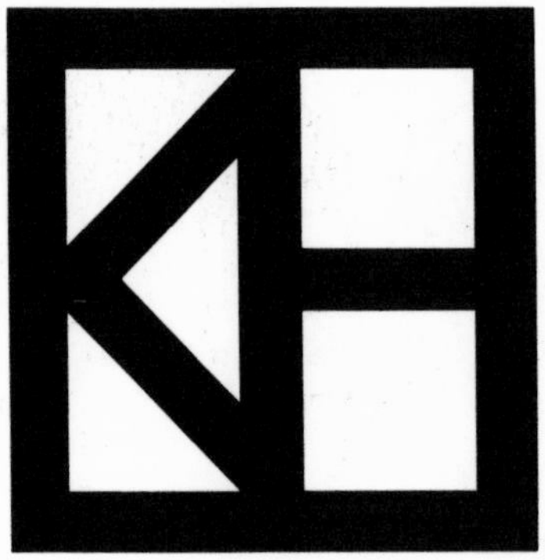

199

200

201

202

203

204

205

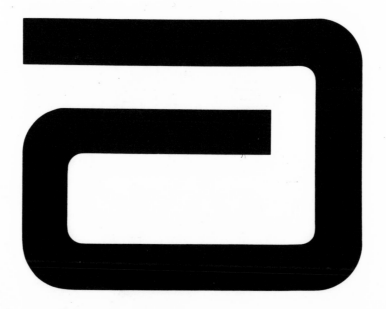

206

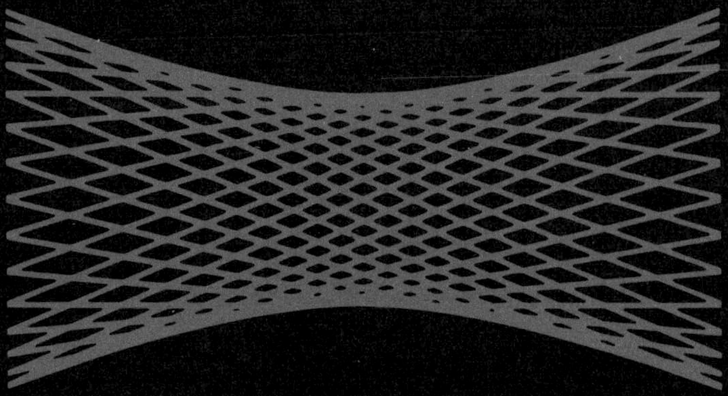

207

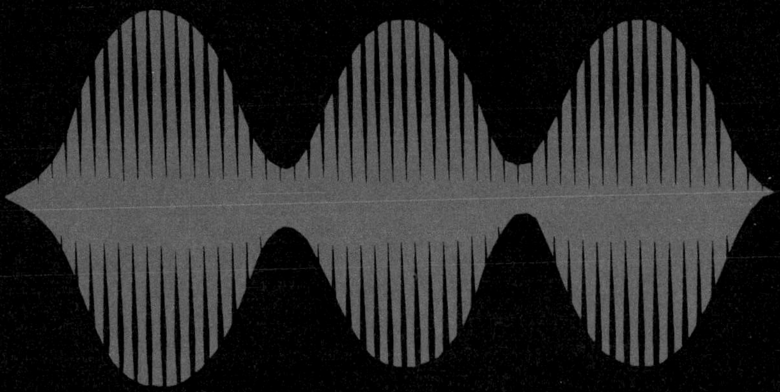

208

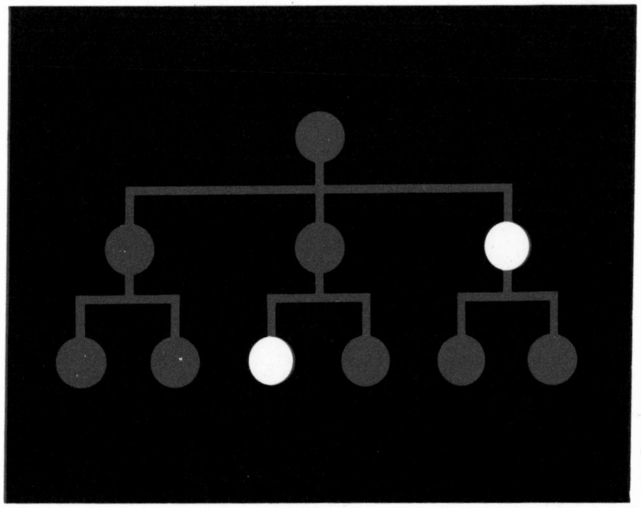

209

Habitat

210

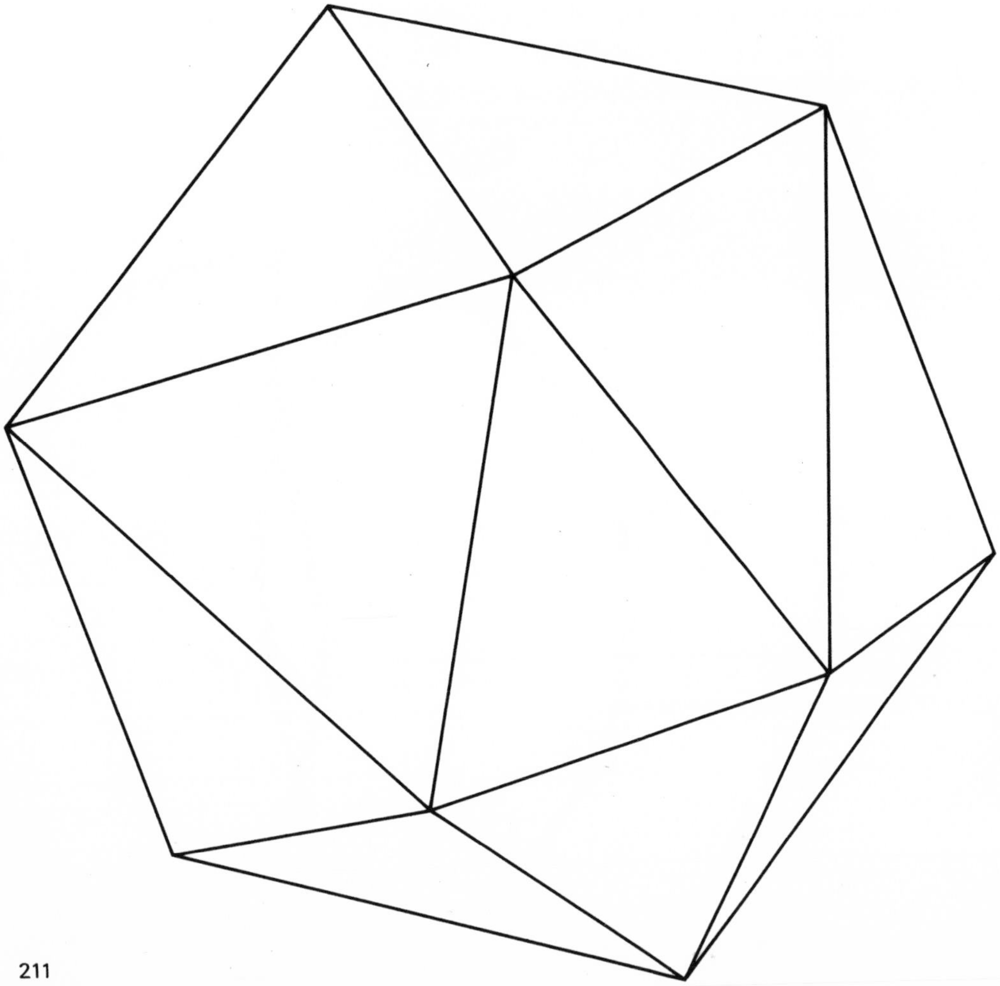

211

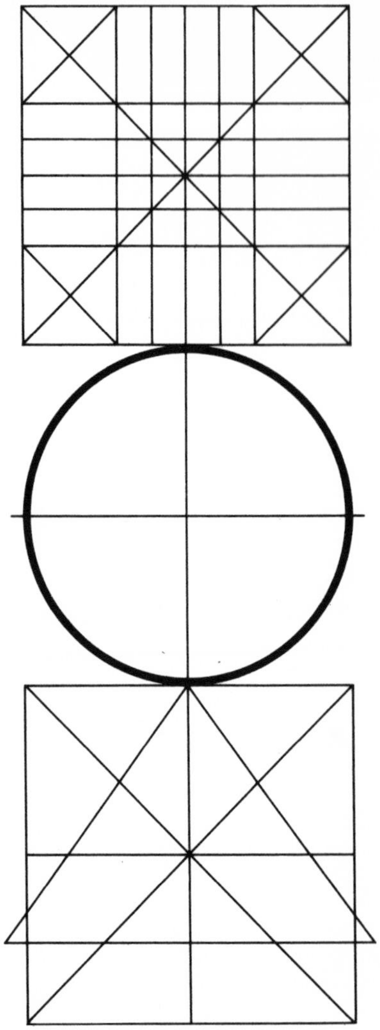

212

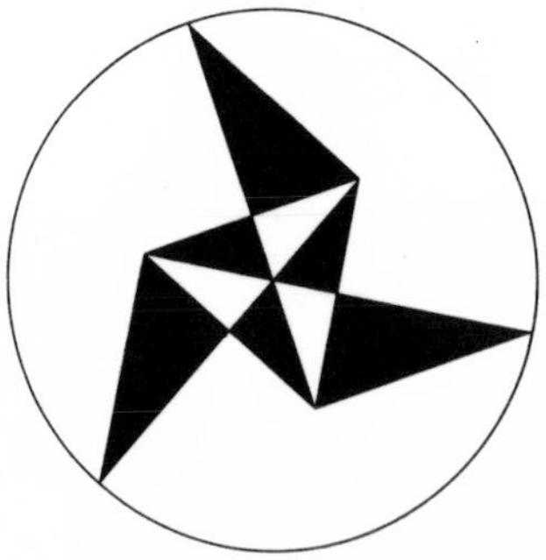

213

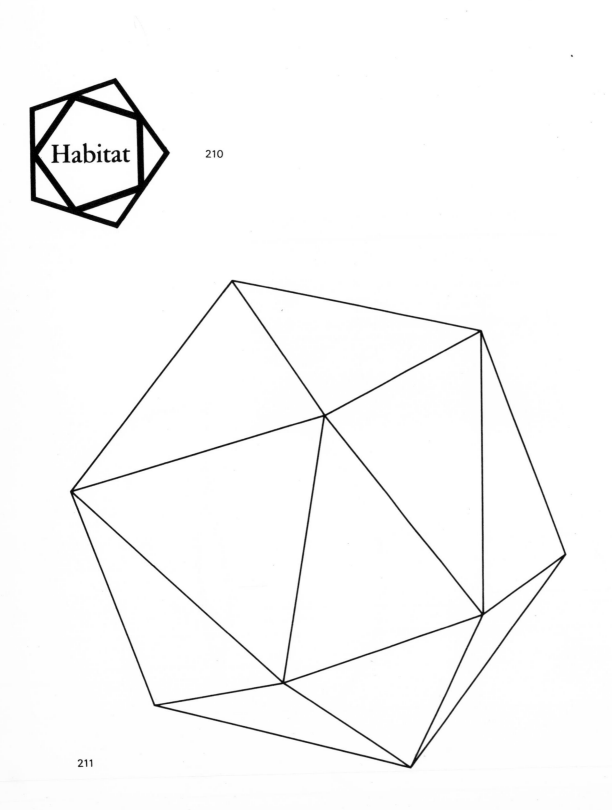

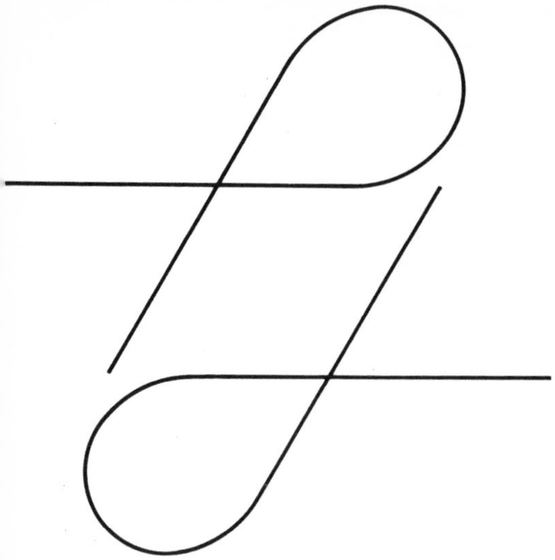

214

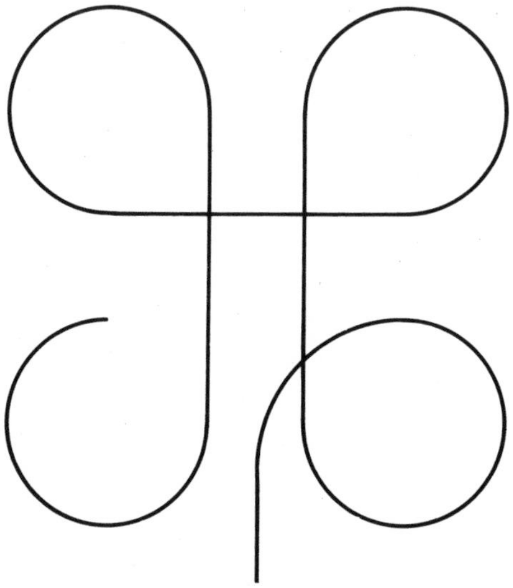

215

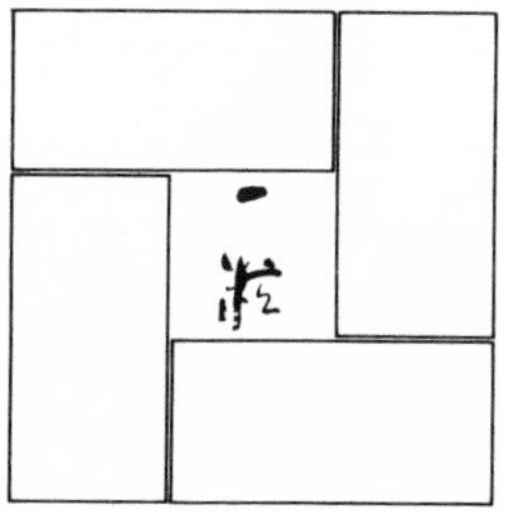

216

217

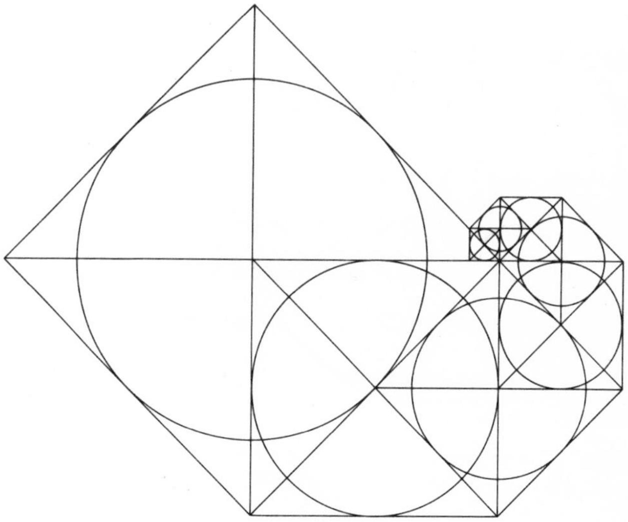

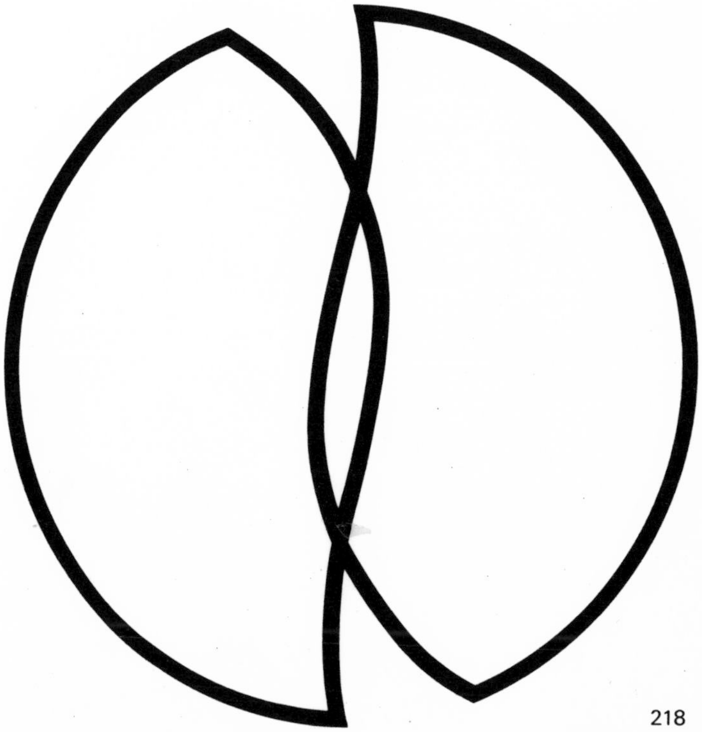

218

EROS

LIAISON

219

220

221

222

HARRIDGE'S

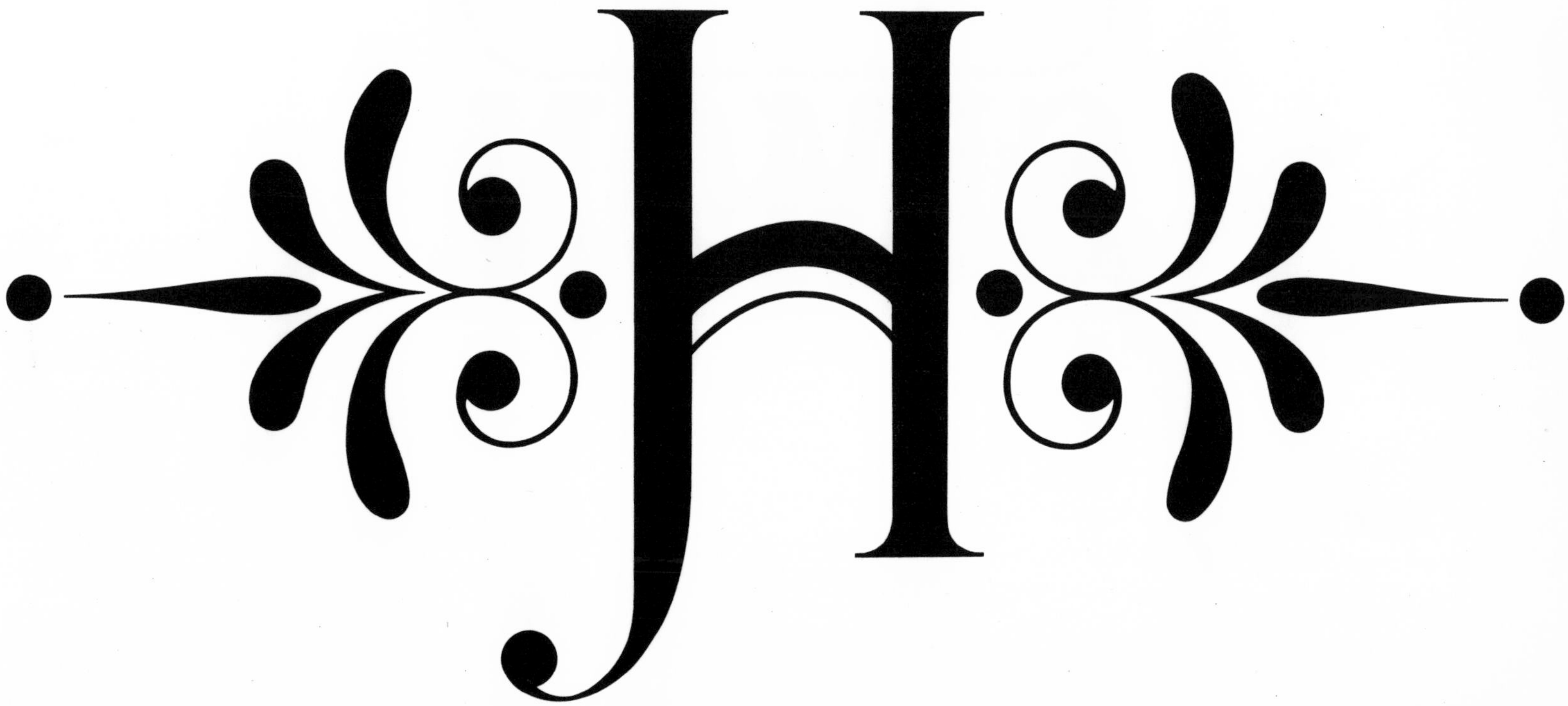

Franklin

SIMON

223

224

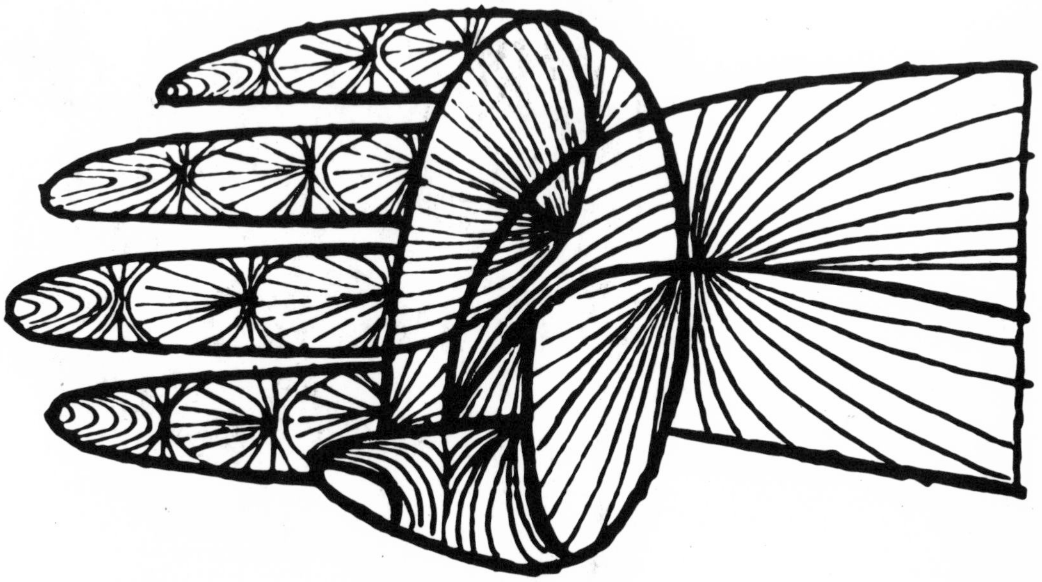

225

226

227

228

SULZER

229

Vitam

230

231

232

233

234

235

236

237 WATNEYS

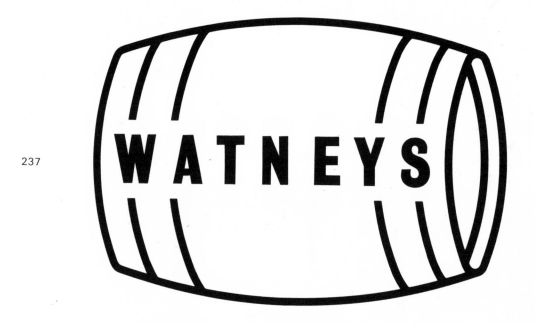

238 dunlop

239

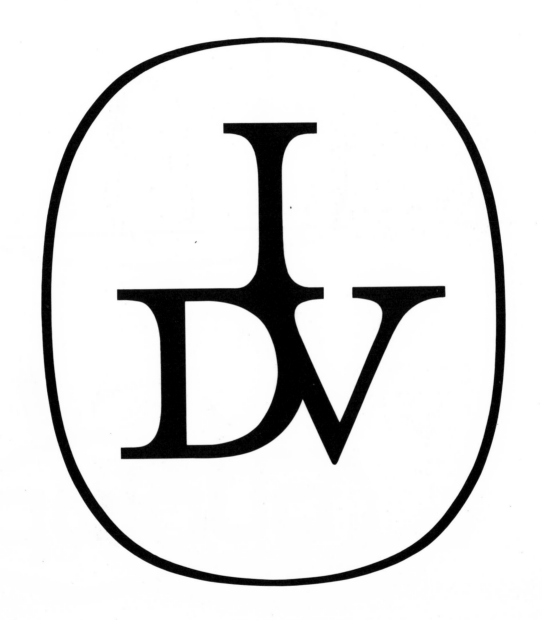

240

241

242

243

Alhambra
MAURICE CHEVALIER

244

THÉÂTRE
TNP
NATIONAL POPULAIRE

245

246

247

248

249 250

251 252

253 254

255

256

257

259

258

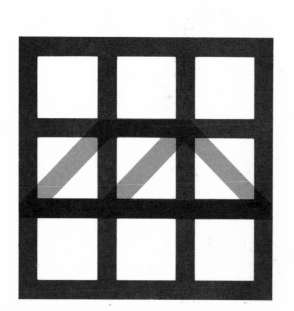

260

261

262

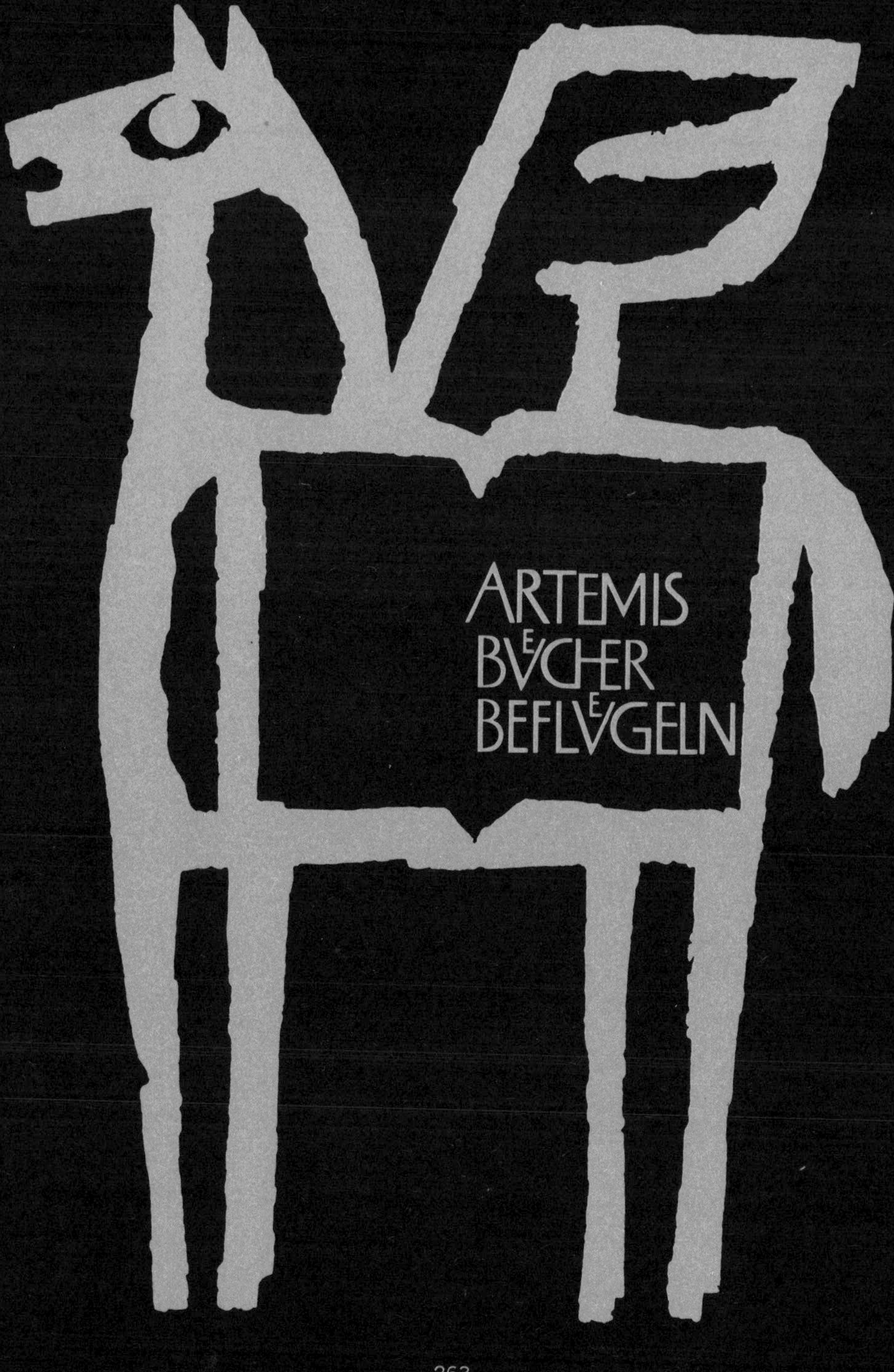

263

264

265

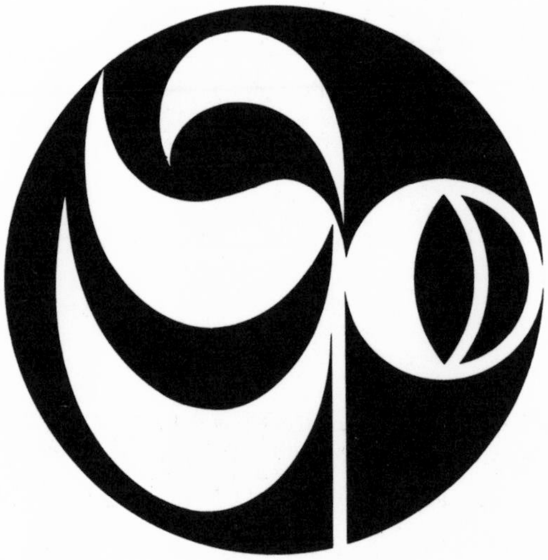

266

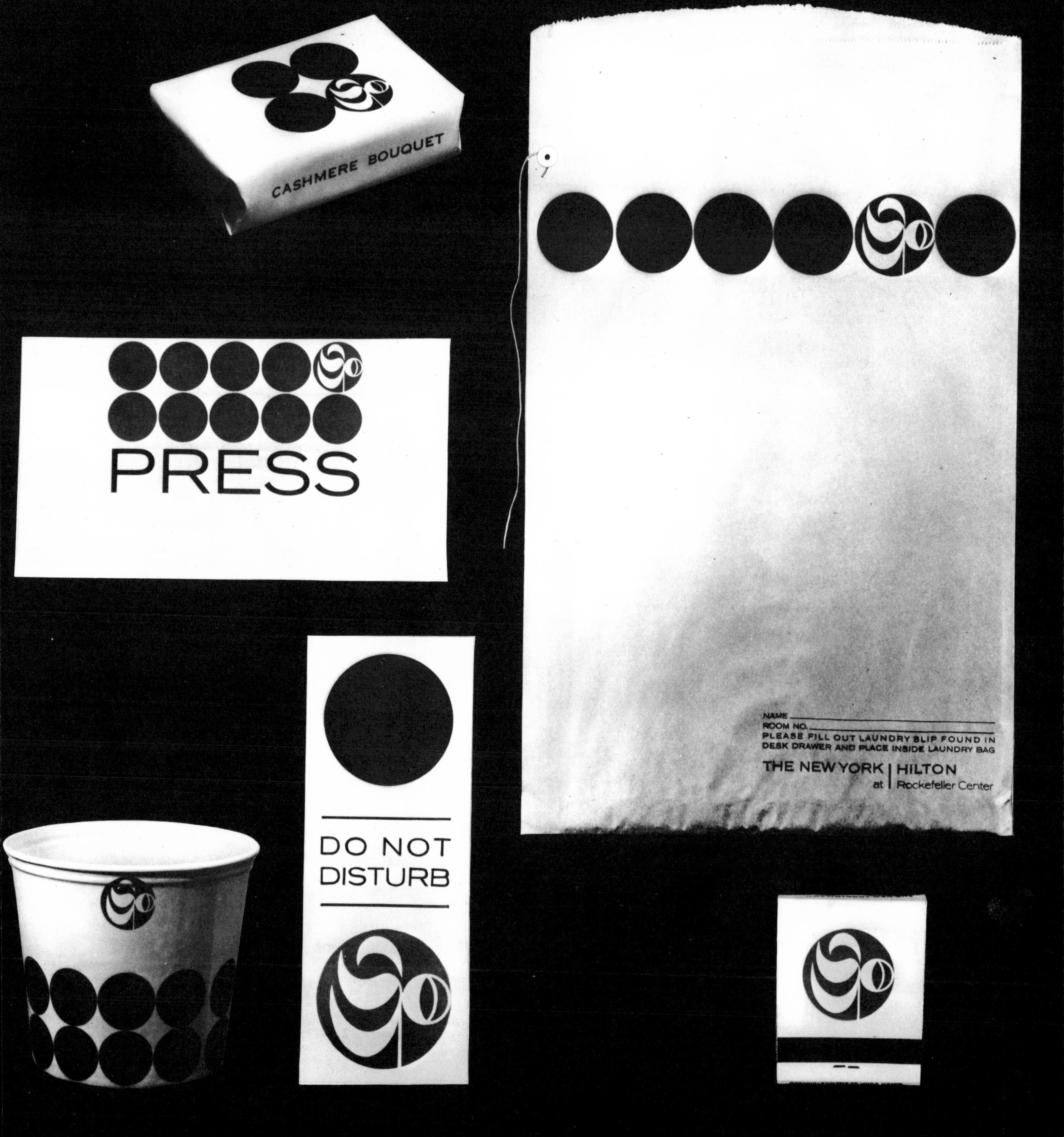
CASHMERE BOUQUET
PRESS
NAME
ROOM NO.
PLEASE FILL OUT LAUNDRY SLIP FOUND IN
DESK DRAWER AND PLACE INSIDE LAUNDRY BAG
THE NEW YORK | HILTON
at | Rockefeller Center
DO NOT
DISTURB

LAWRY'S

268

270

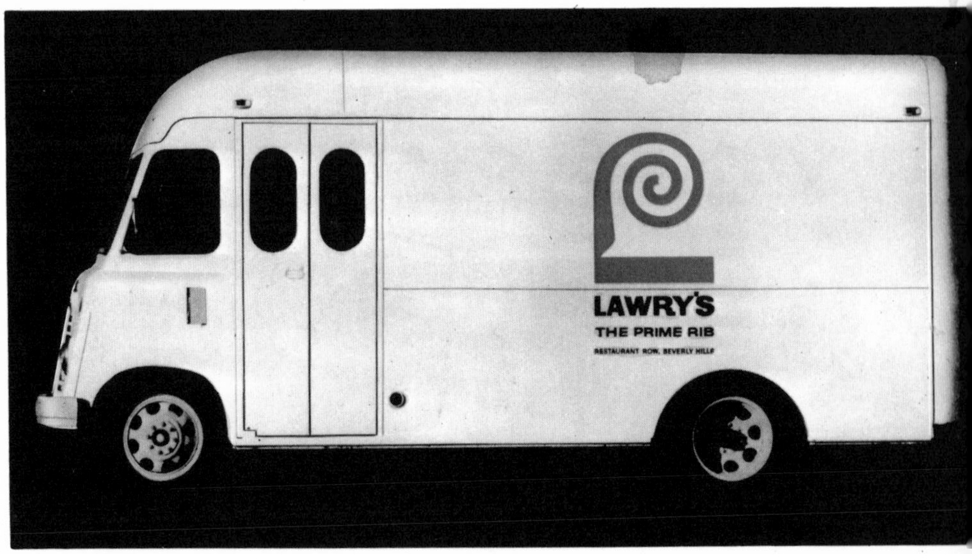

269

titeflex

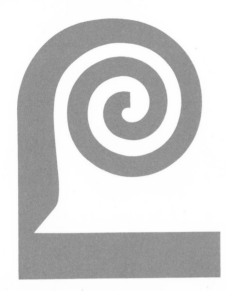

274

271

272

273

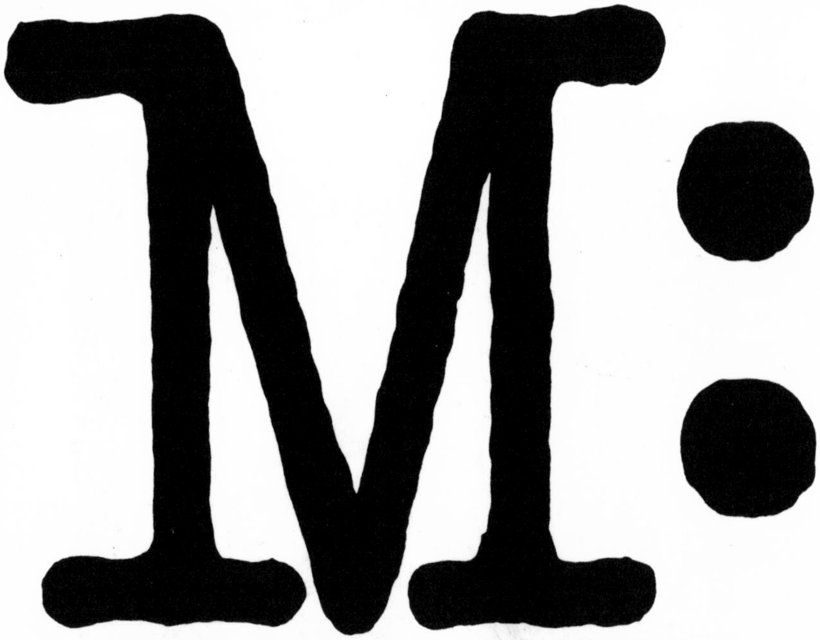

275

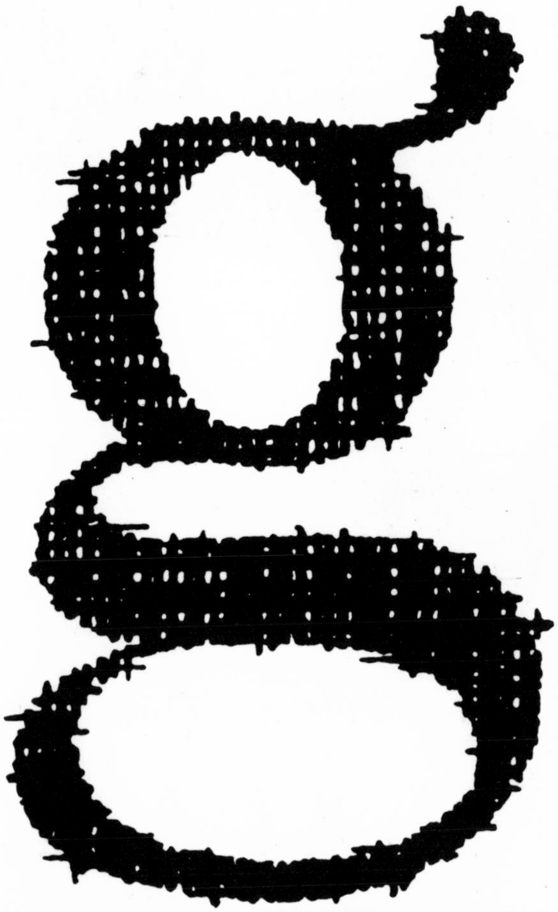

276

277

278

Ditto

279

280

Westinghouse Light Bulbs
60 watt
50 watt
40 watt
50¢
Westinghouse
Control

281

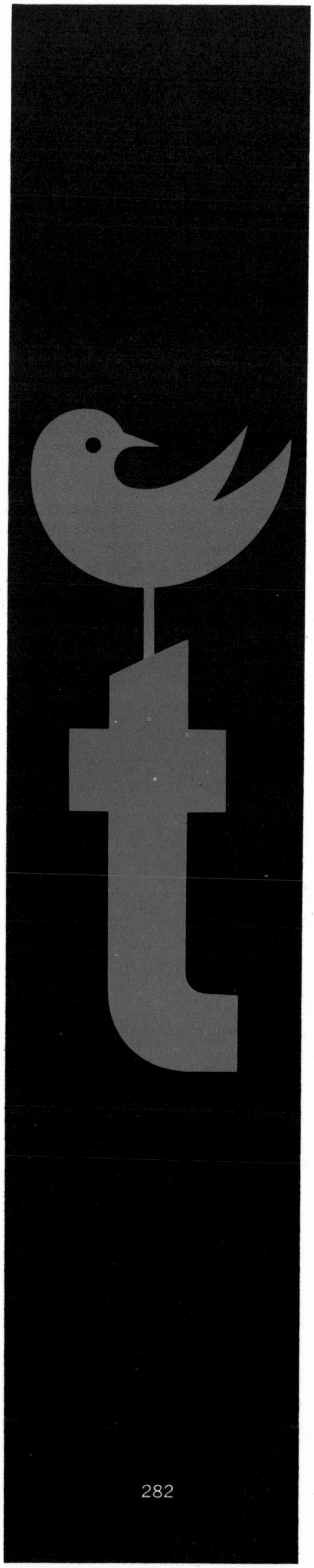
282

283

284

285

286

287

288

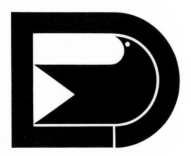

289

290

291

292

293

294

295

296

297

298

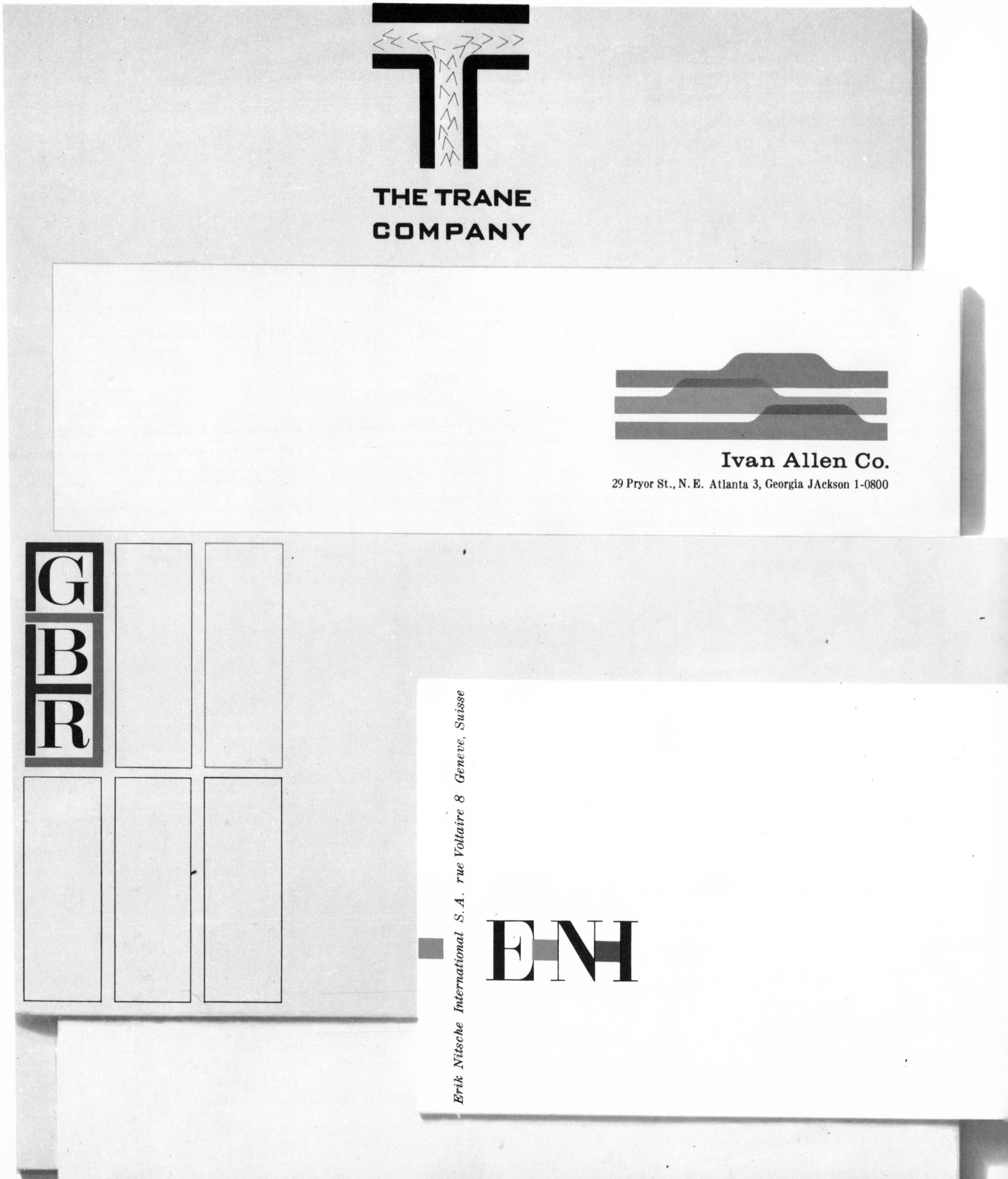

299

300

301

302

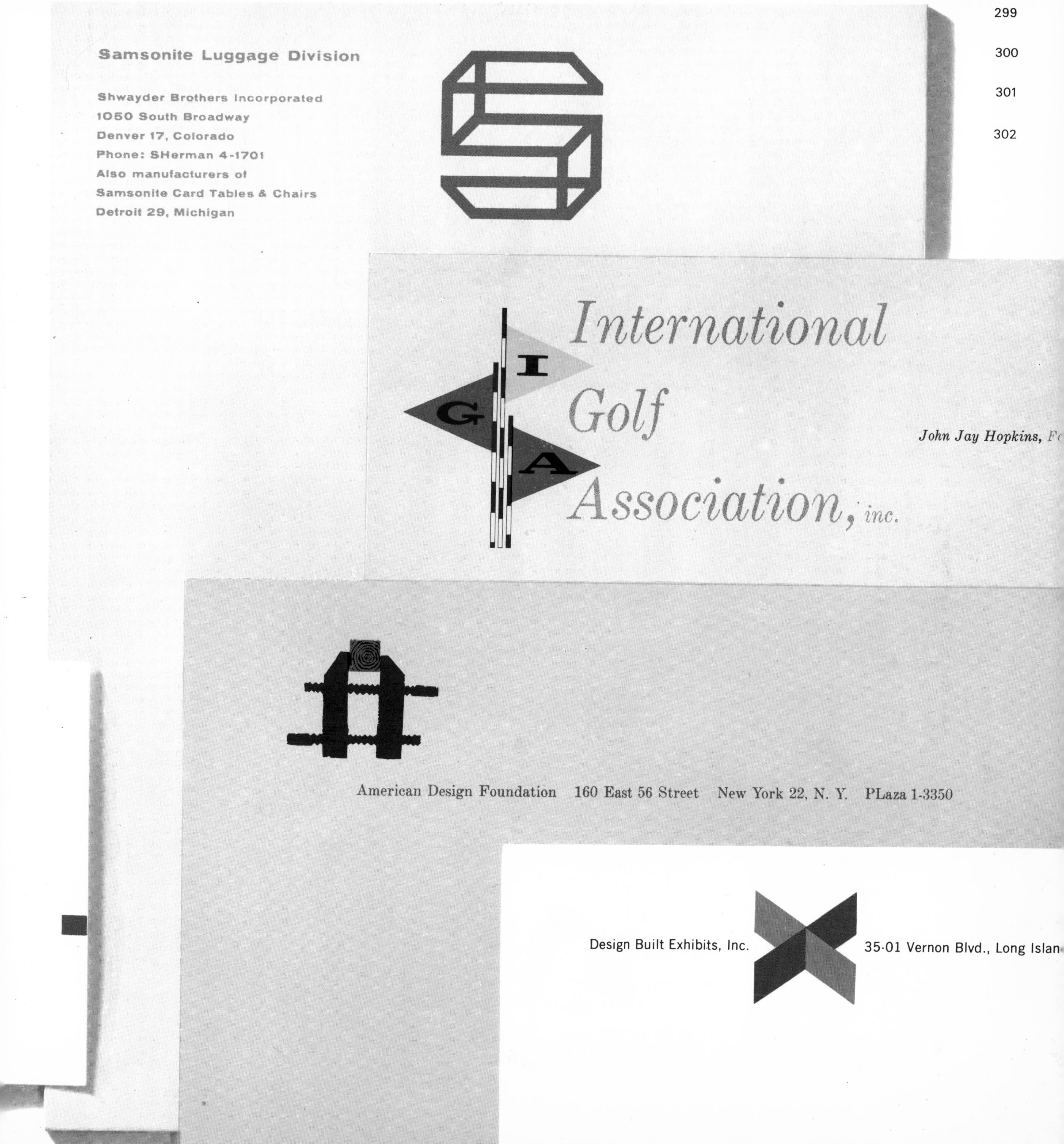

Samsonite Luggage Division
Shwayder Brothers Incorporated
1050 South Broadway
Denver 17, Colorado
Phone: SHerman 4-1701
Also manufacturers of
Samsonite Card Tables & Chairs
Detroit 29, Michigan
I G A
International Golf Association, inc.
John Jay Hopkins, F
American Design Foundation 160 East 56 Street New York 22, N. Y. PLaza 1-3350
Design Built Exhibits, Inc.
35-01 Vernon Blvd., Long Islan

CCA

303

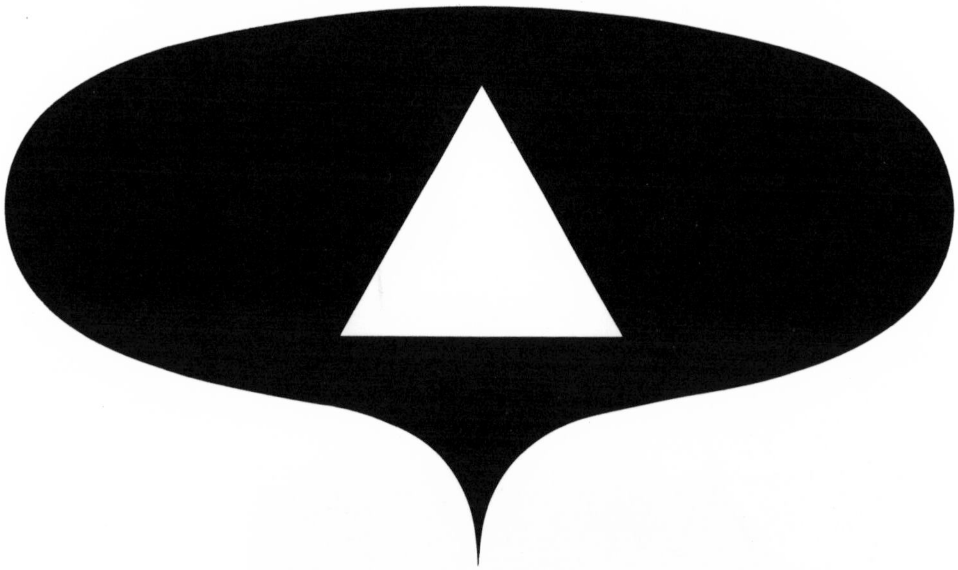

304

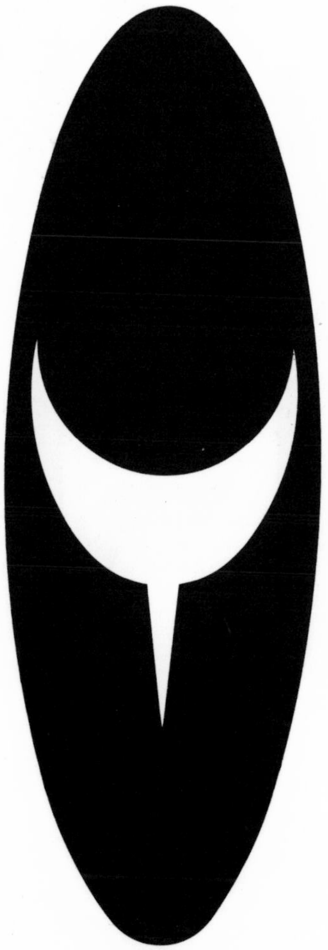

305

306

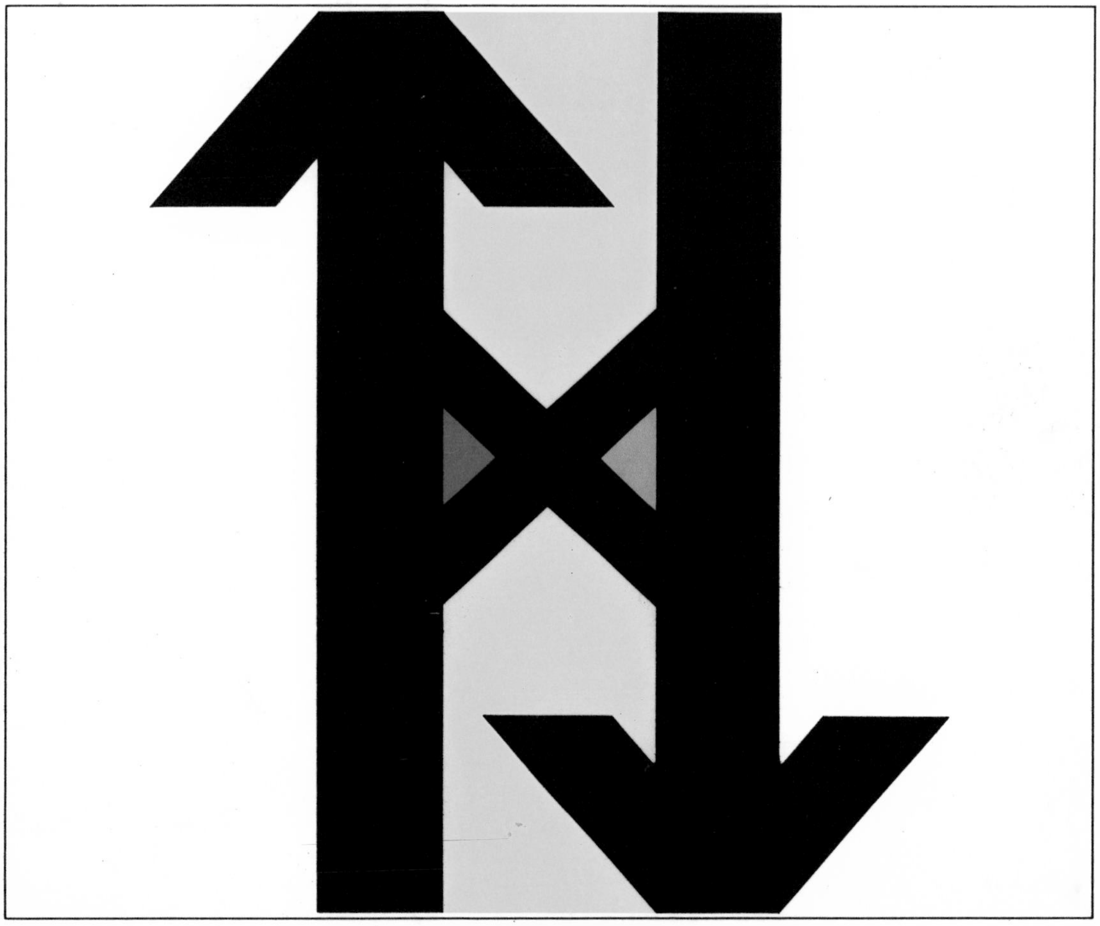

307

308

309

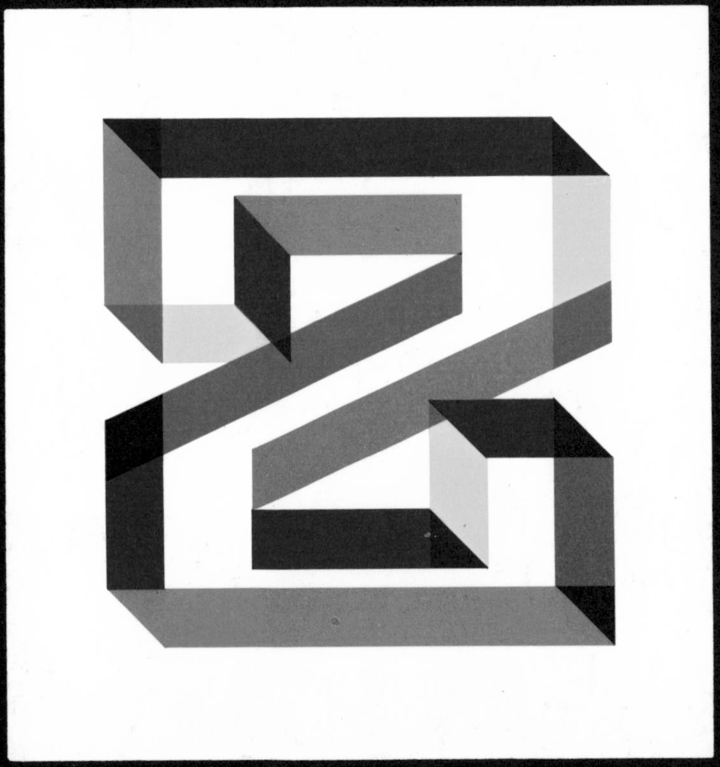

310

311

312

313

315

314

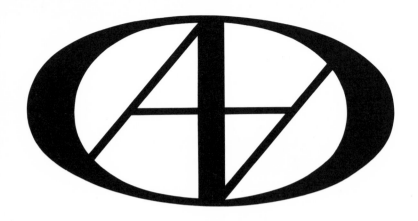

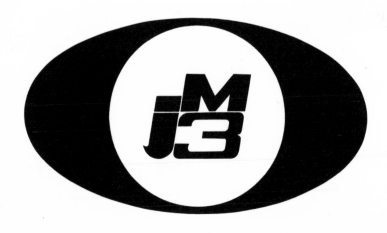

316

317

318

319

320

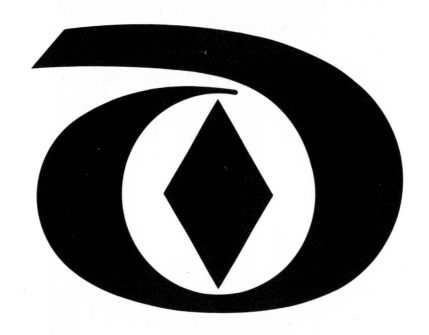

321

322

323

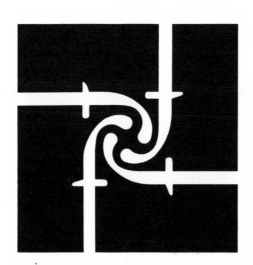

324

327

330

325

328

326

329

331

332

ŒRTLI

333

334

335

336

337

339

341

343

338

340

342

344

347

349

348

350

345

346

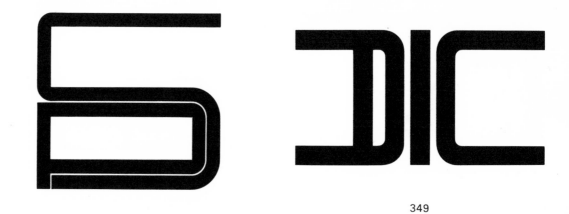

351

352

353

354

355

356

357

358

359

360

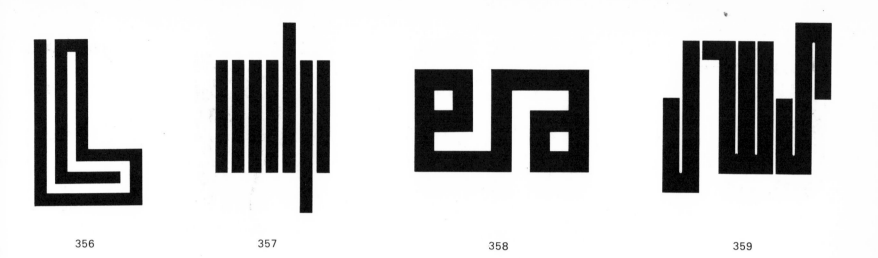

361

364

367

GALVANITE

362

365

368

363

366

scei

369

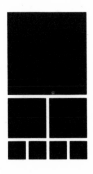

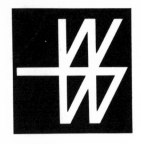

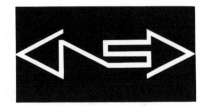

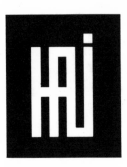

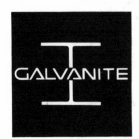

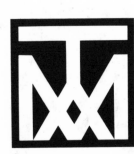

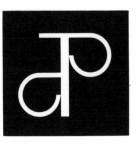

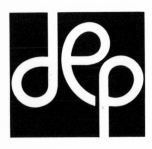

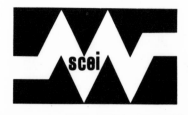

370

371

372

373

374

375

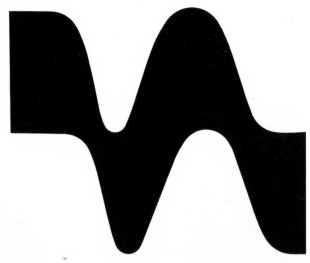

NOLAND PAPER COMPANY, INC.

376

377

378

379

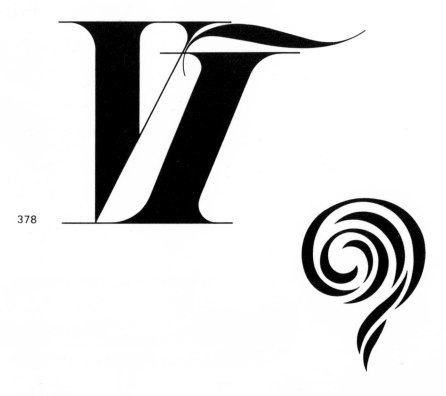

380

381

382

383

384

385

391

392

386

389

393

387

394

388

390

397

398

401

395

399

402

396

400

403

404

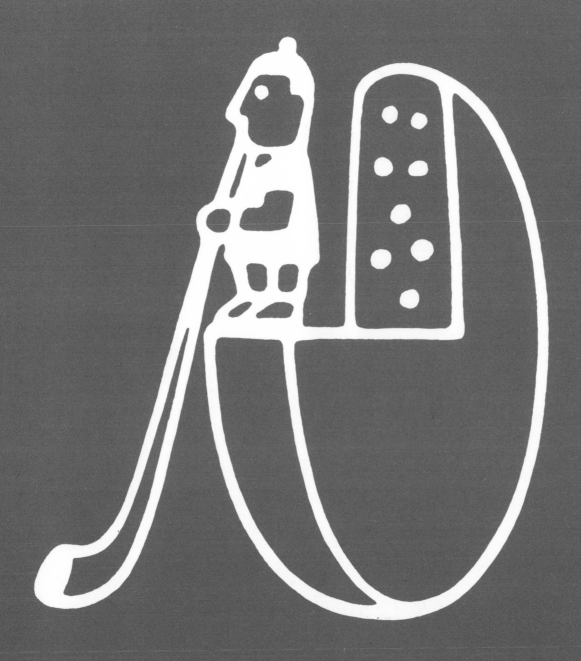

405

406

407

408

409

410

411

412

413

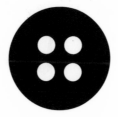

414

415

416

417

418

419

420

421

422

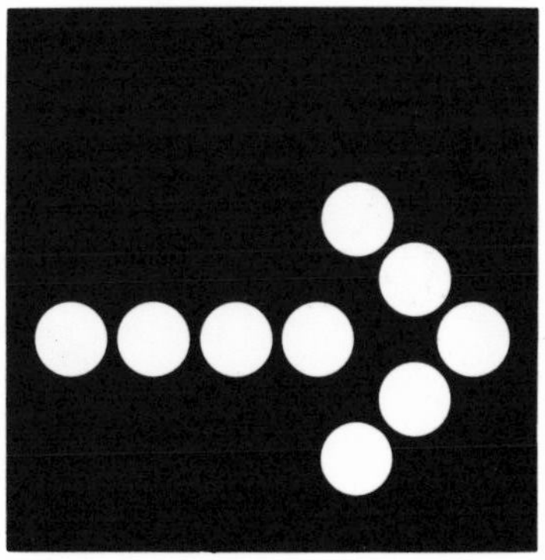

423

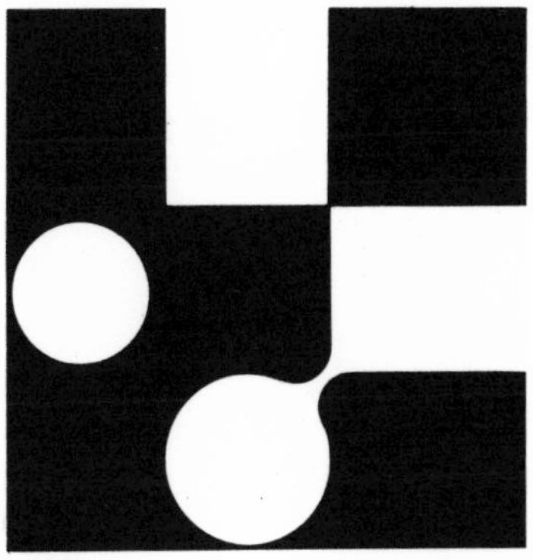

424

425

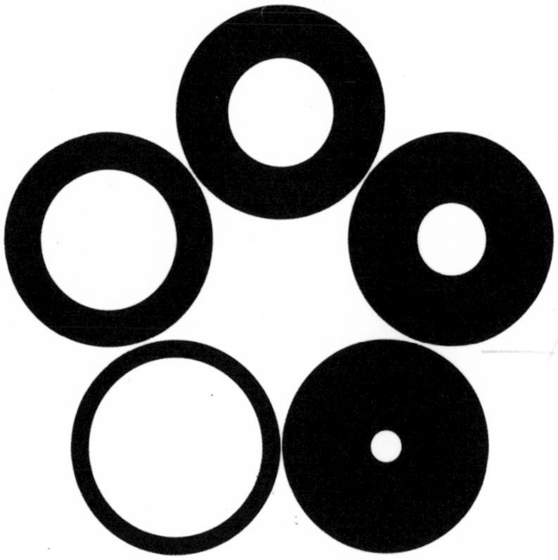

426

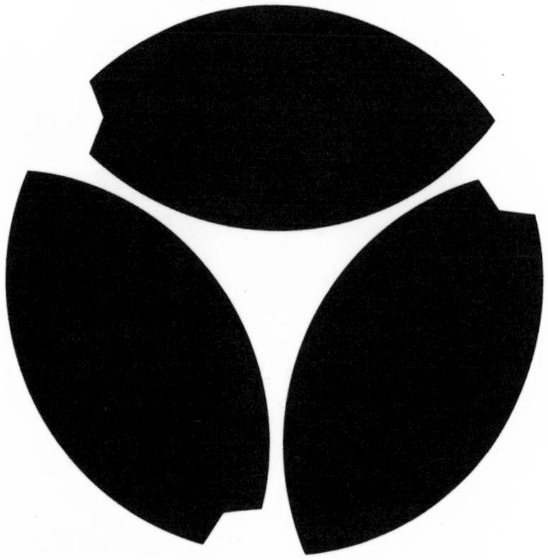

427

428

429

430

431

432

433

434

435

436

437

438

439

440

441

442

443

444

445

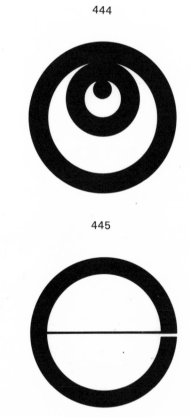

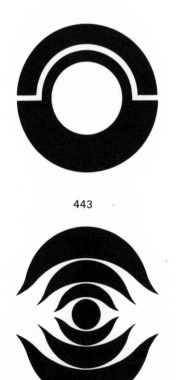

450

446

448

447

449

451

452

454

453

455

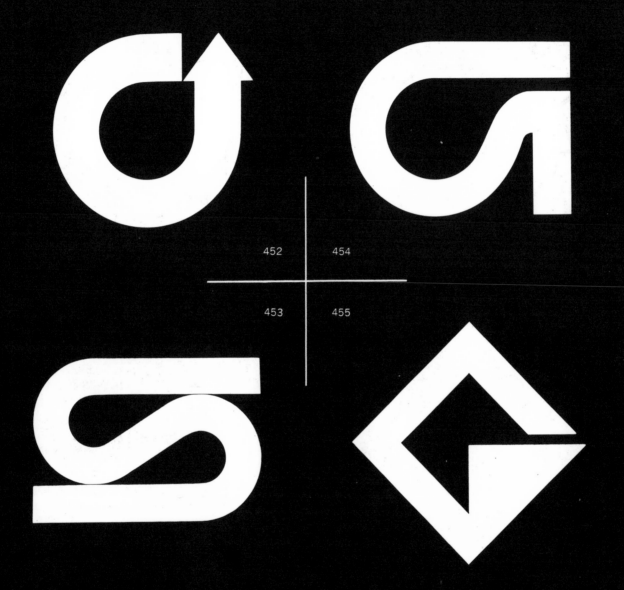

456

458

457

459

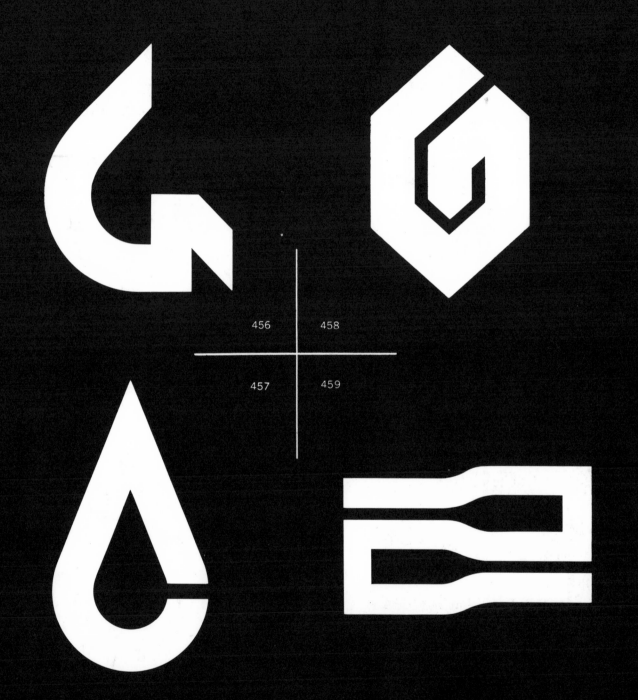

EQUITABLE

460

THE LARK BY STUDEBAKER

461

sangiorgio

462

463

SB &H SALOMON BROTHERS & HUTZLER

464

PANAVIEW SLIDING ALUMINUM DOORS

465

466 ESTON

chairmasters 467

Packaging 468

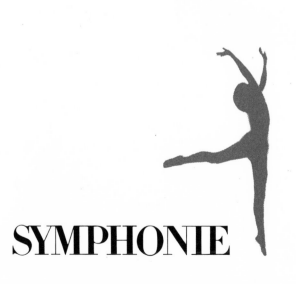

469 SYMPHONIE

470

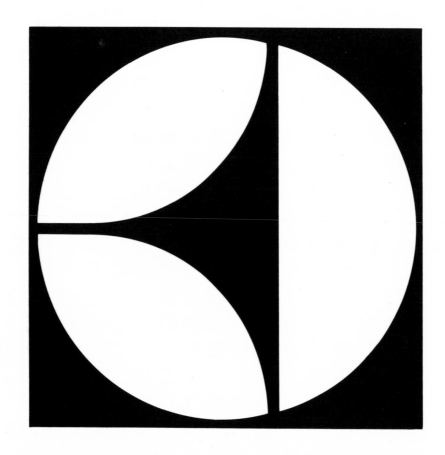

471

472

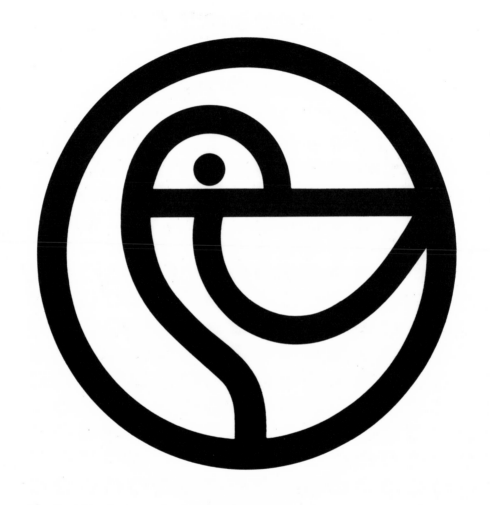

ESCHER
WYSS

473

474

475

476

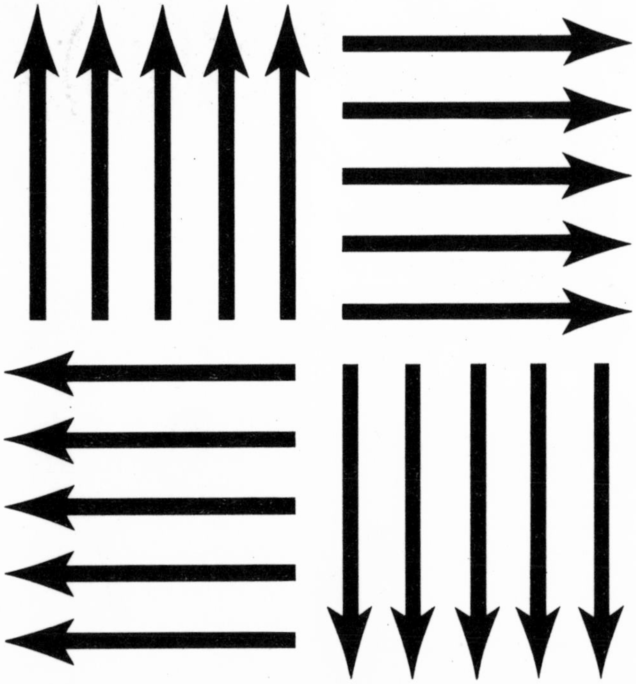

477

478

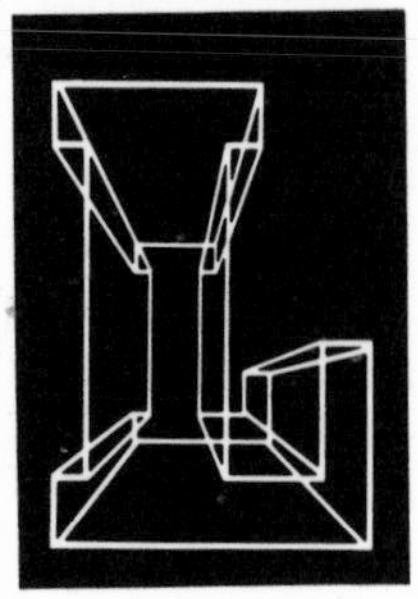

479

480

CAPROTTI

481

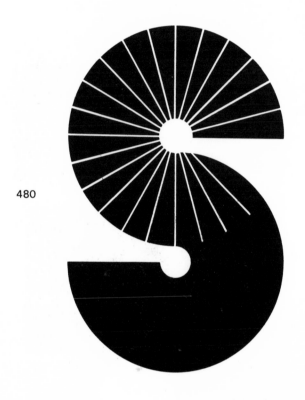

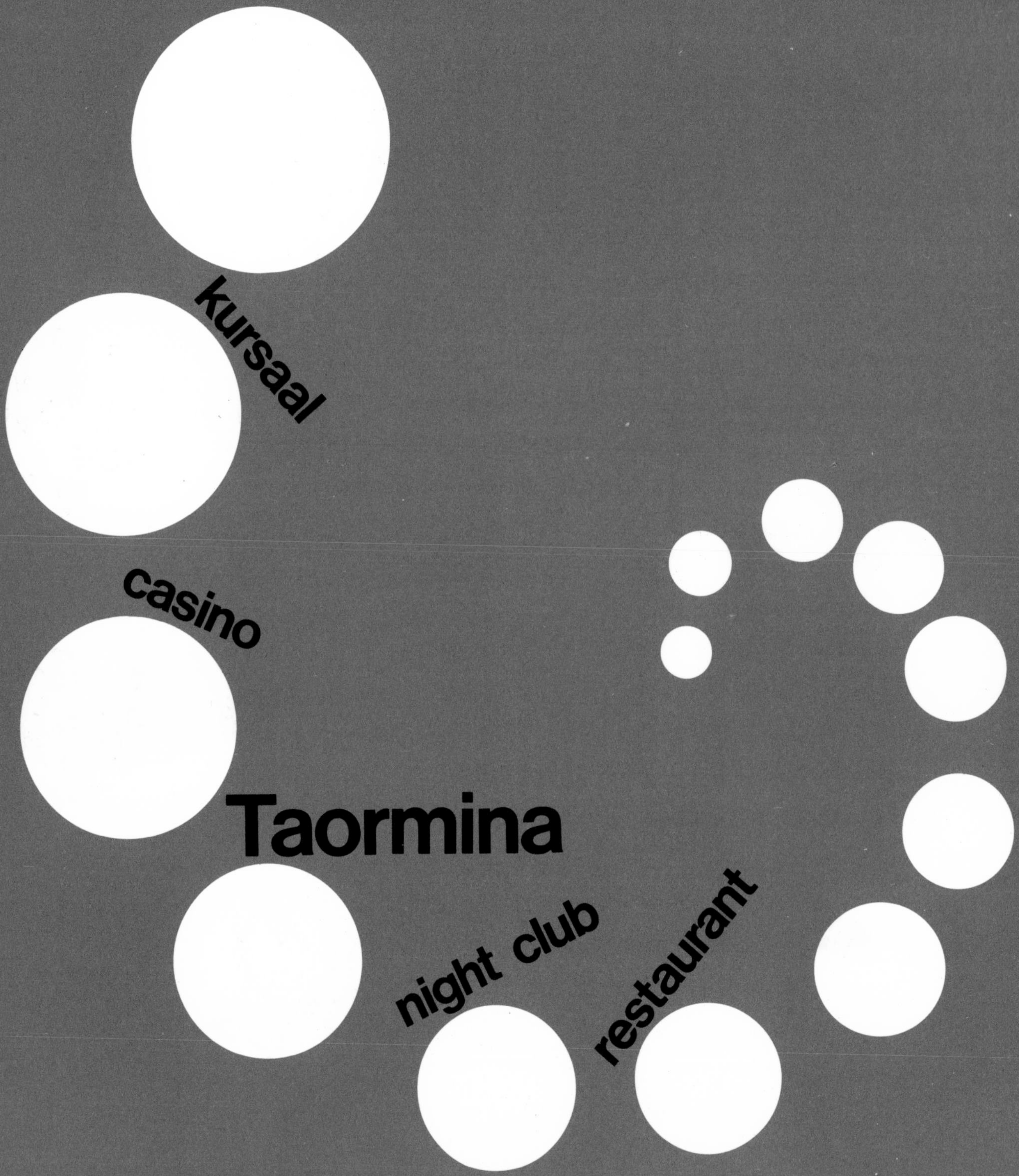

482

483

484

485

486

487

488

489

490

496

491

492

493

494

495

ALCOA

497

498

499

500

501

502

503

504

505

506

507

513

508 509 510 511 512

514

516

515

517

519

518

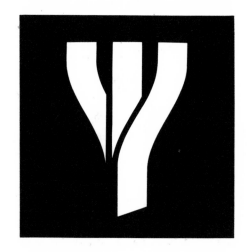

521

520

522

524

523

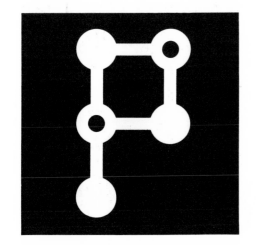

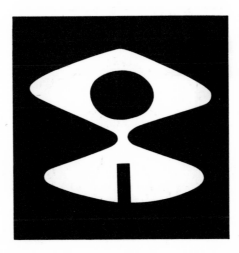

525

526

532

527

533

528

534

529

535

530

536

531

537

538

539

540

541

542

543

544

545

546

547

548

549

550

551

552

553

554

555

556

557

558

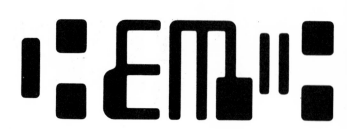

magnum

559

560

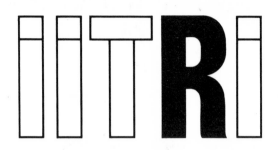

Westinghouse

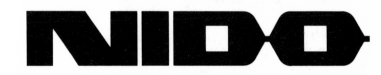

iiTRi

561

562

NIDO

563

564

565

566

567

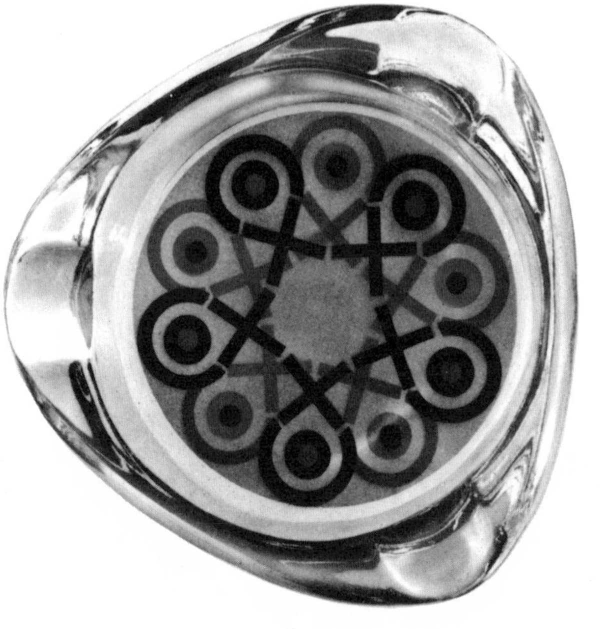

568

569

570

bilia

571

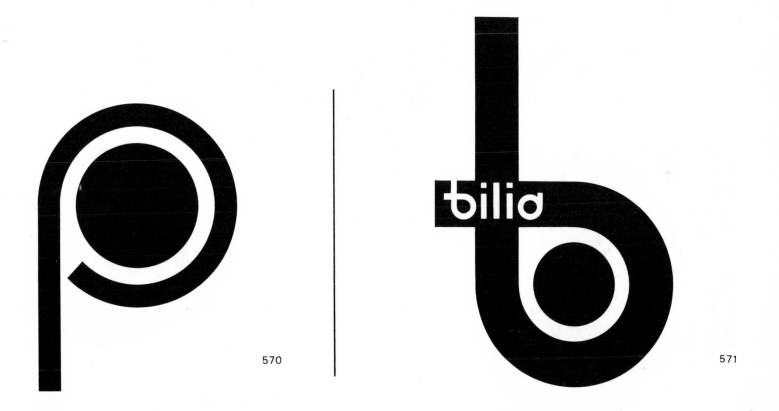

572

THE
MAN
WITH
THE
GOLDEN
ARM

574

SPARTACUS

573

OTTO PREMINGER PRESENTS
ADVISE
&CONSENT

575

576

577

578

579

580 —— 585

WESTMINSTER WINE

586

A R

587

588

589

590

591

RIZZI

TELEFONO 22456 BORDIGHERA

VIA VITTORIO EMANUELE 251

592

FORNASETTI ORIGINALS

596

INTARSIO

597

CITTA' DI CARTE

593

BUONI BOCCONI

598

TIRO A SEGNO

594

MEDAGLIONI NELL'OTTAGONO

595

Sirene

FORNASETTI · MILANO

MADE IN ITALY

599

CANI

600

FORNASETTI MILANO
MADE IN ITALY

601

SCULTORI
ITALIANI

602

ASSI

603

TEMA E
VARIAZIONI

604

ASTROLABIO

605

IL MONDO
ALLA ROVESCIA

606

STOVIGLIE
FORNASETTI
MILANO
MADE IN ITALY
1955

607

FORNASETTI
MILANO - VIA MANZONI 17 - TEL. 860004

608

609

610

611

612

613

614

615

616

617

618

619

620

621

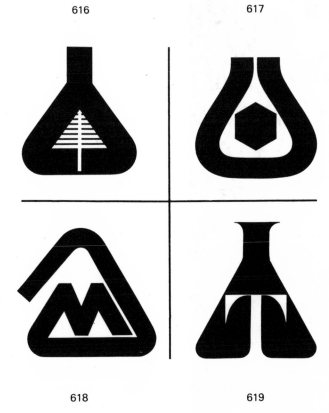

622

623

624

625

626

627

628

629

630

634

637

631

638

633

635

639

632

636

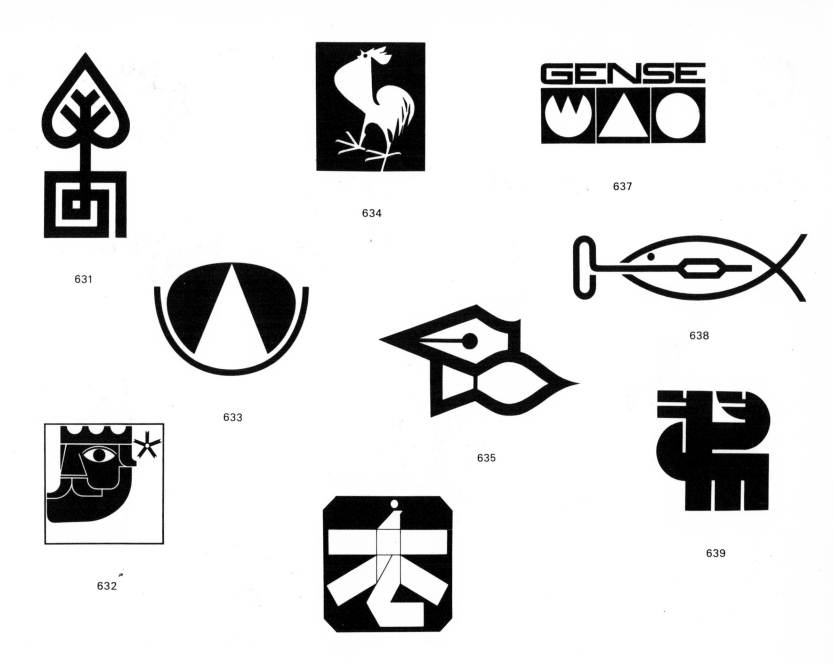

640

641

642

643

644

645

646 —— 676

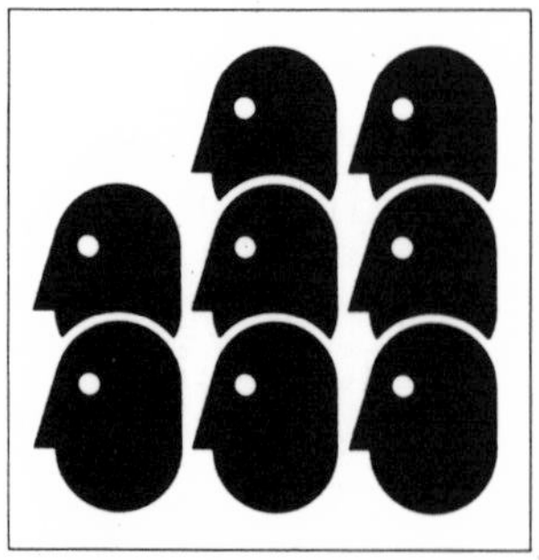

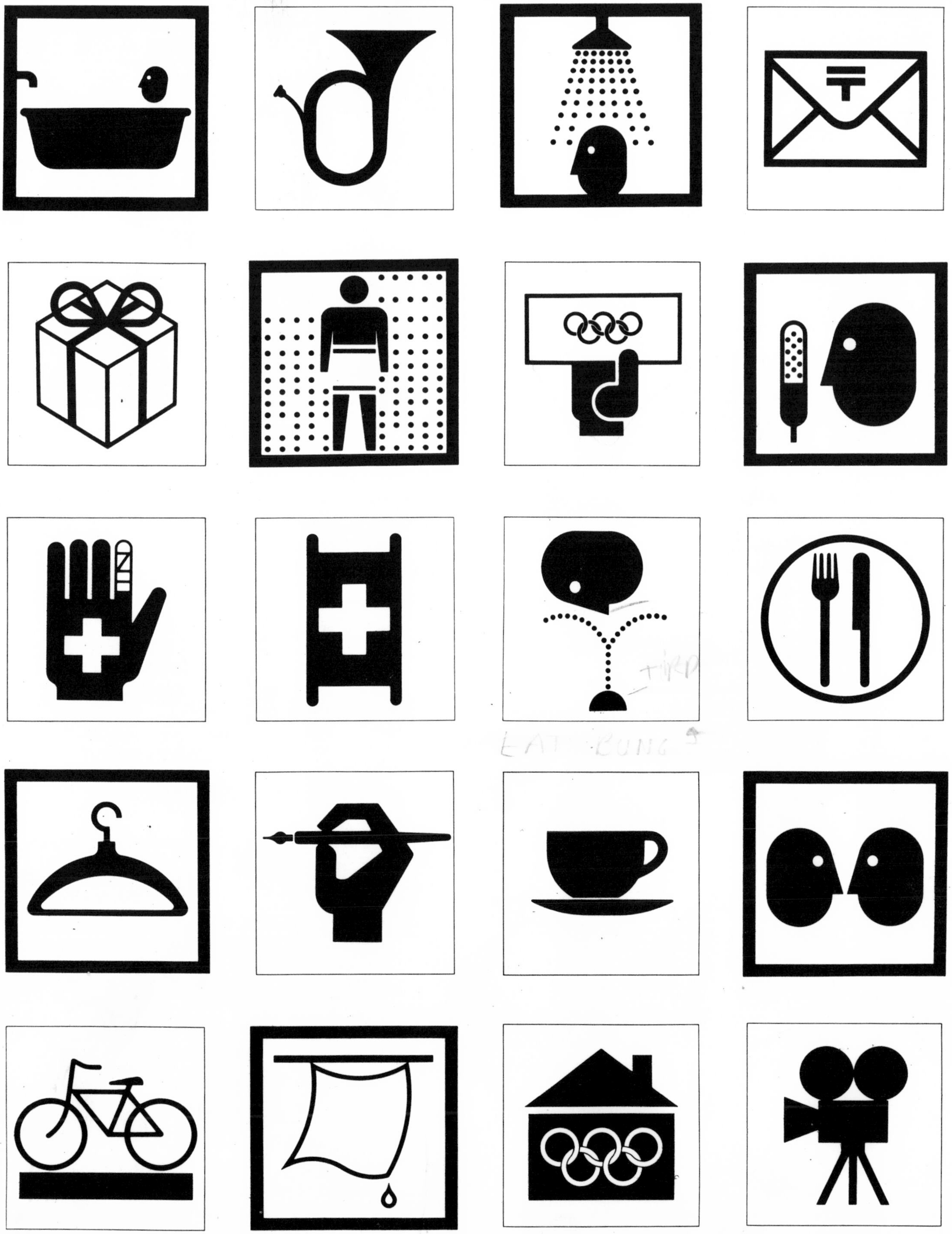

677

678

679

680

681

682

683

684

685

686

687

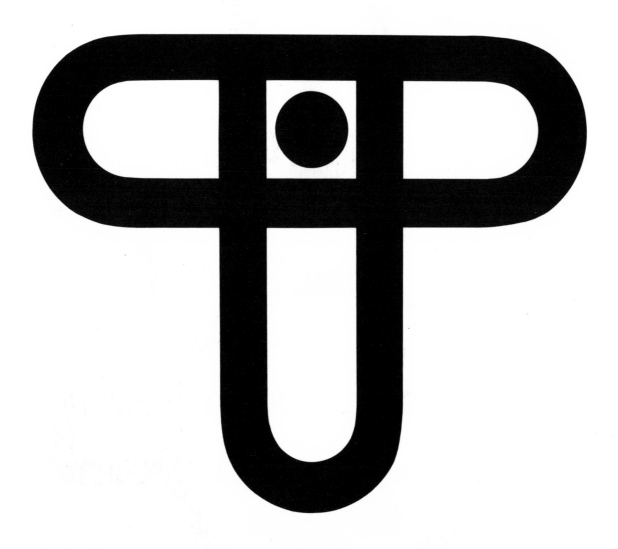

688

689

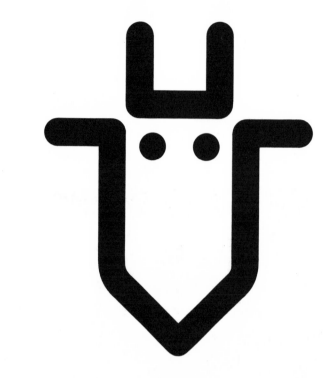

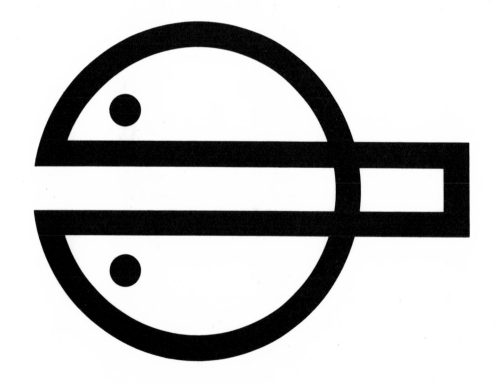

690

691

692

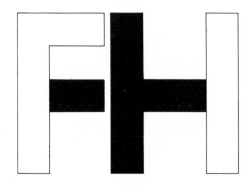

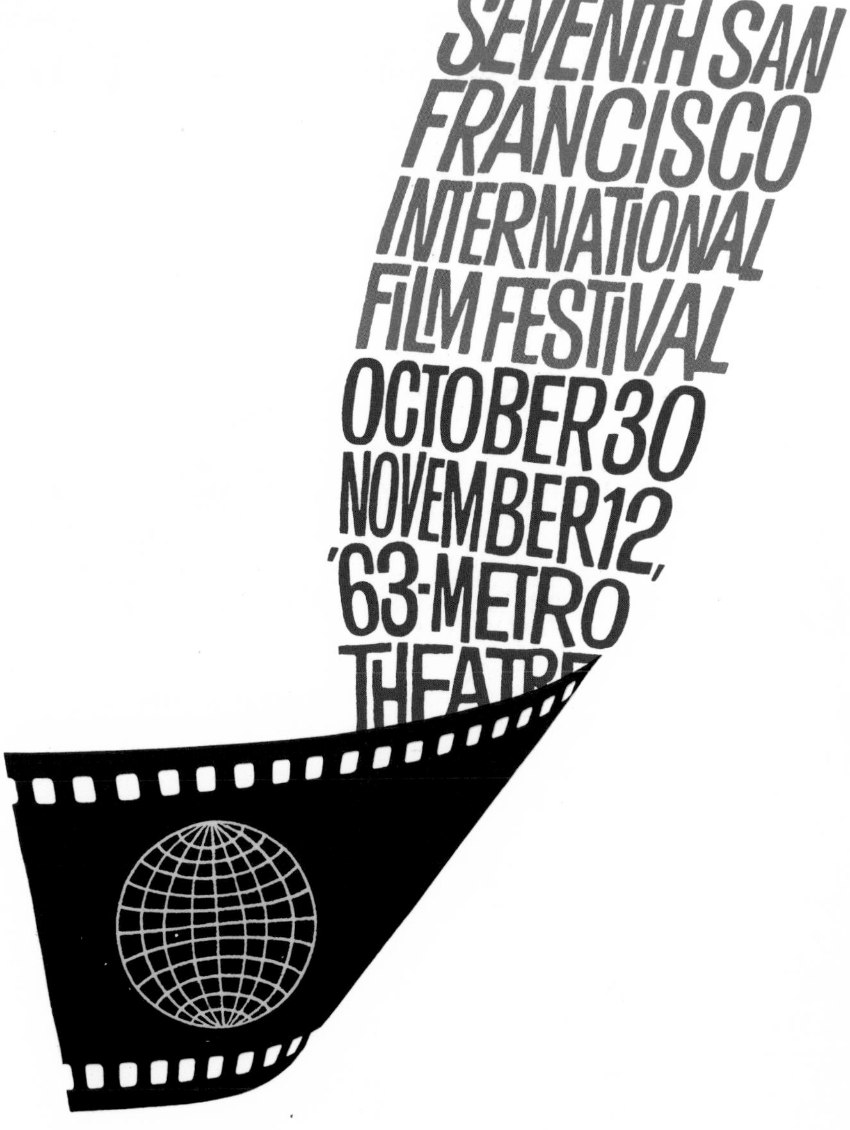
SEVENTH SAN
FRANCISCO
INTERNATIONAL
FILM FESTIVAL
OCTOBER 30
NOVEMBER 12,
'63-METRO

693

negi

694

695

Renggli

GEVACOLOR

696

STONE

697

698

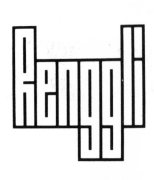

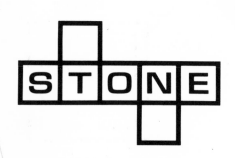

699

700

701

702

703

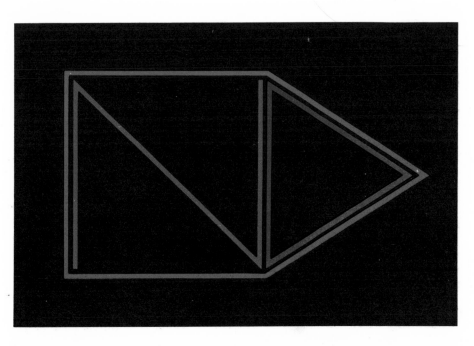

704

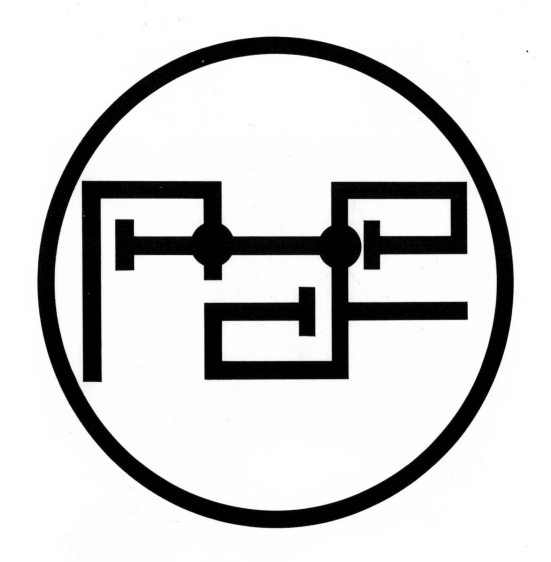

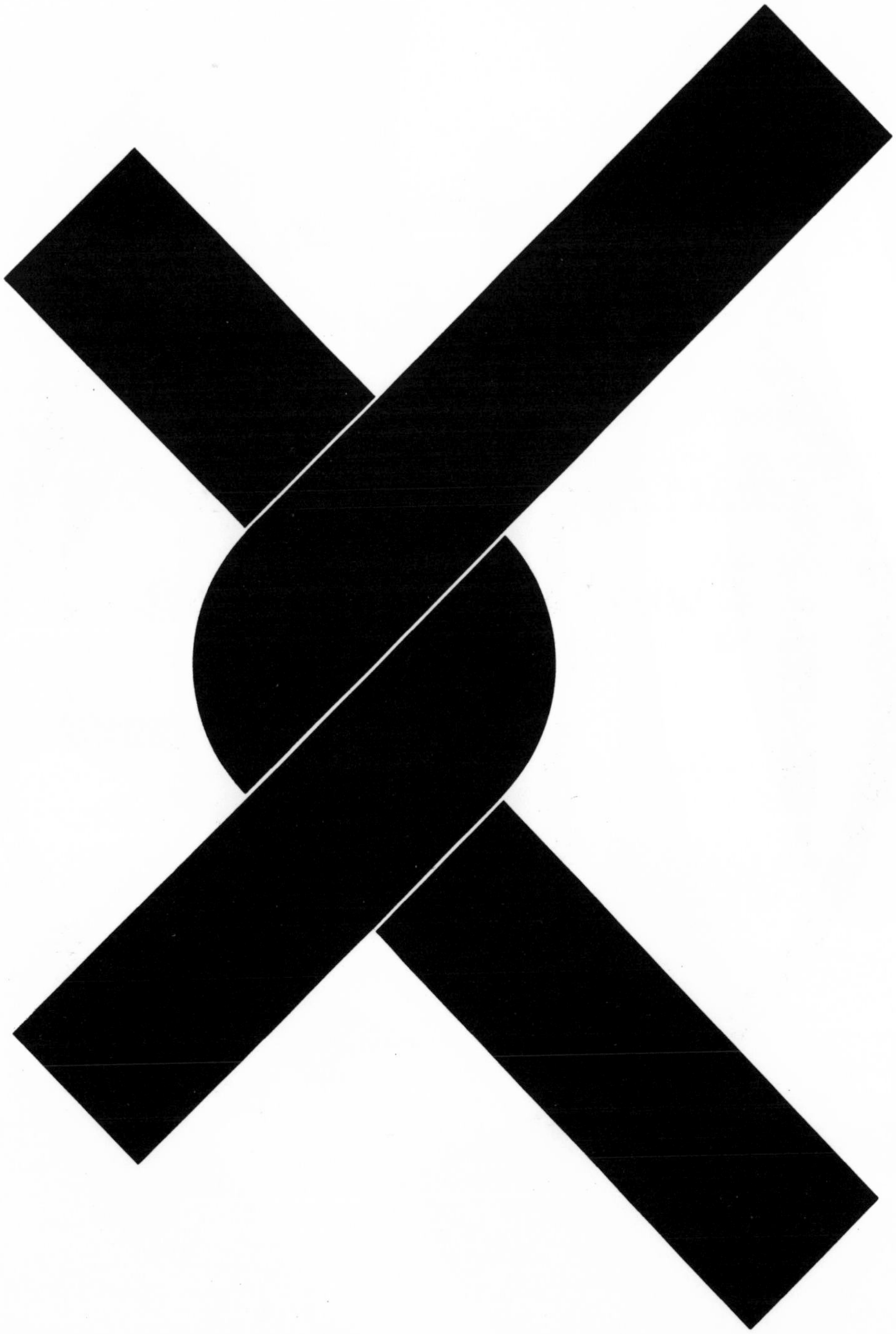

705

706

707

708

709

710

711

712

713

714

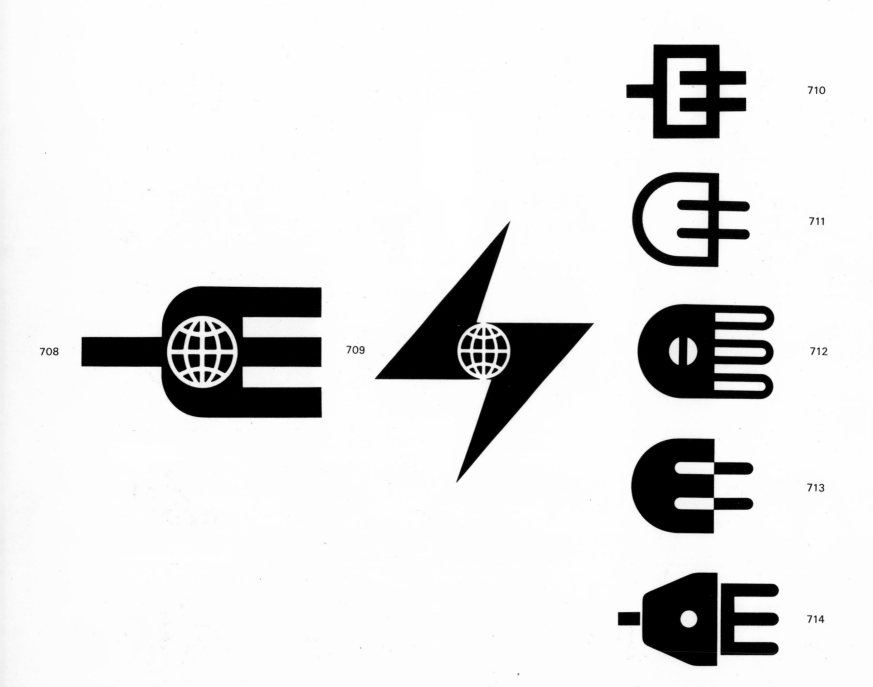

715 —— 734

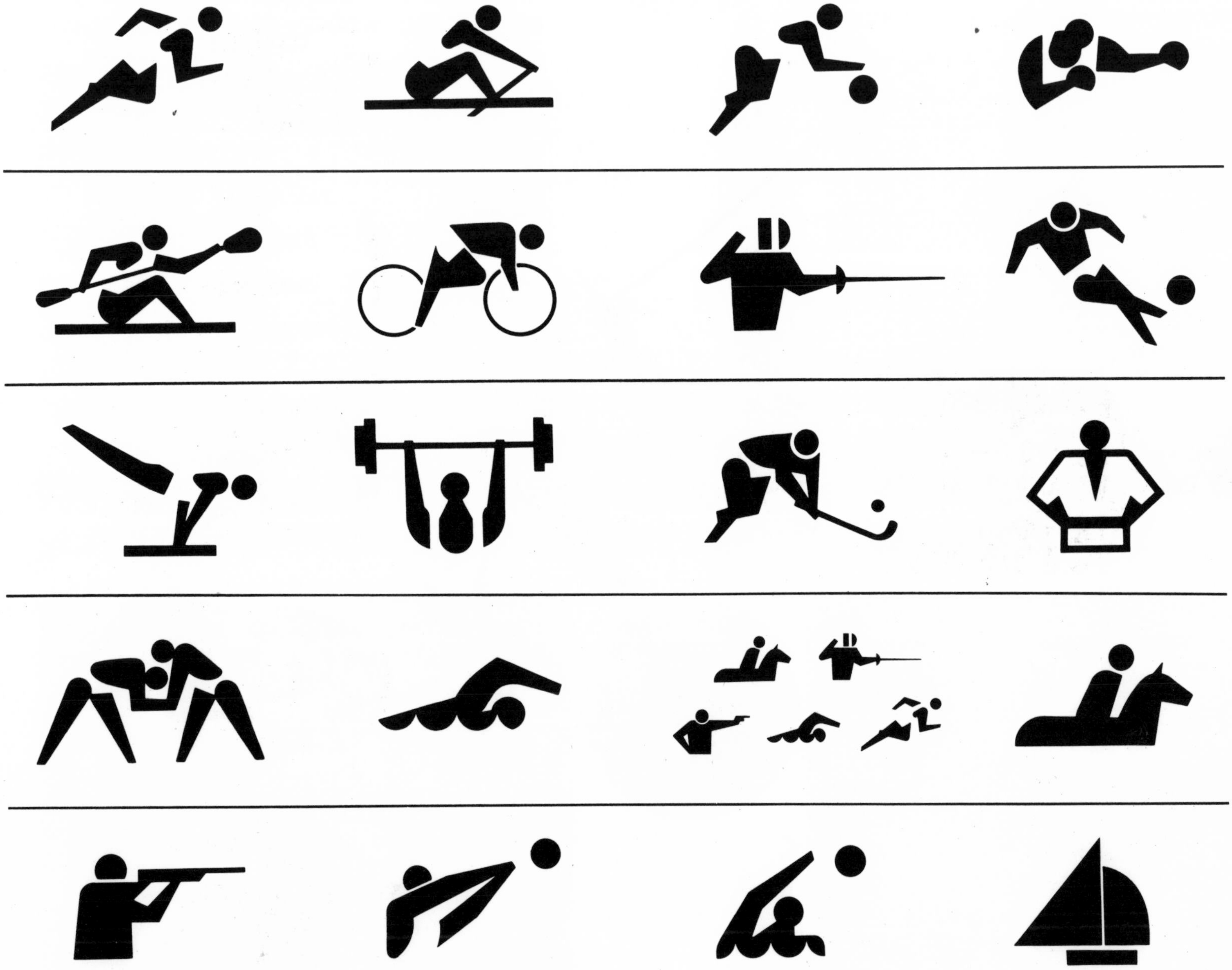

735

736

ombra sol

737

CNLIC

738

739

740

741

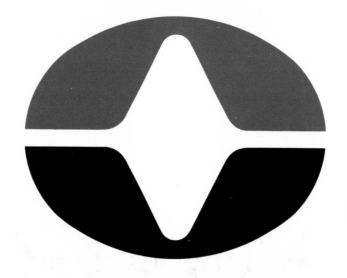

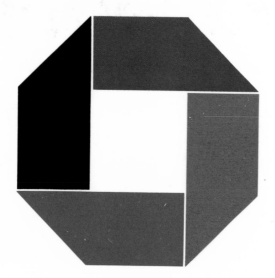

742

743

744

745

746

747

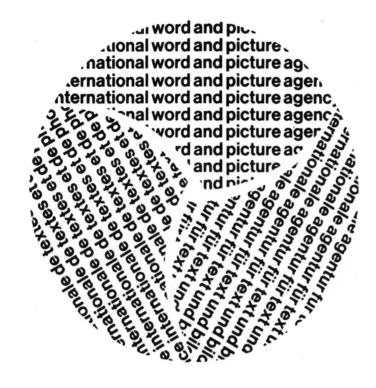

748

749

751

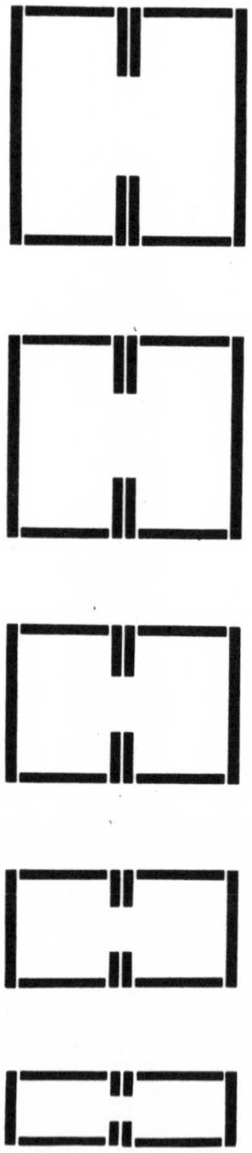

750

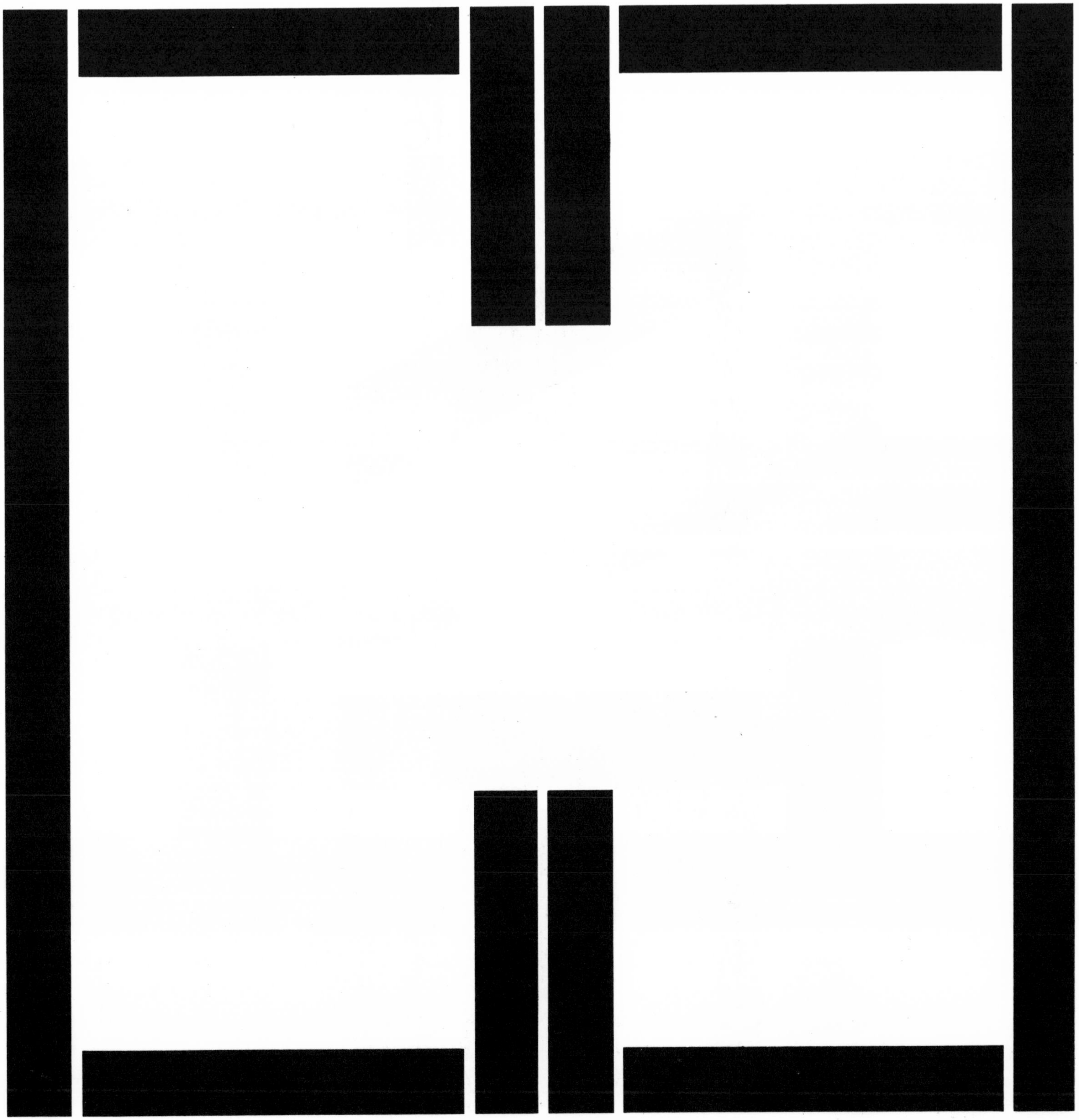

752

753

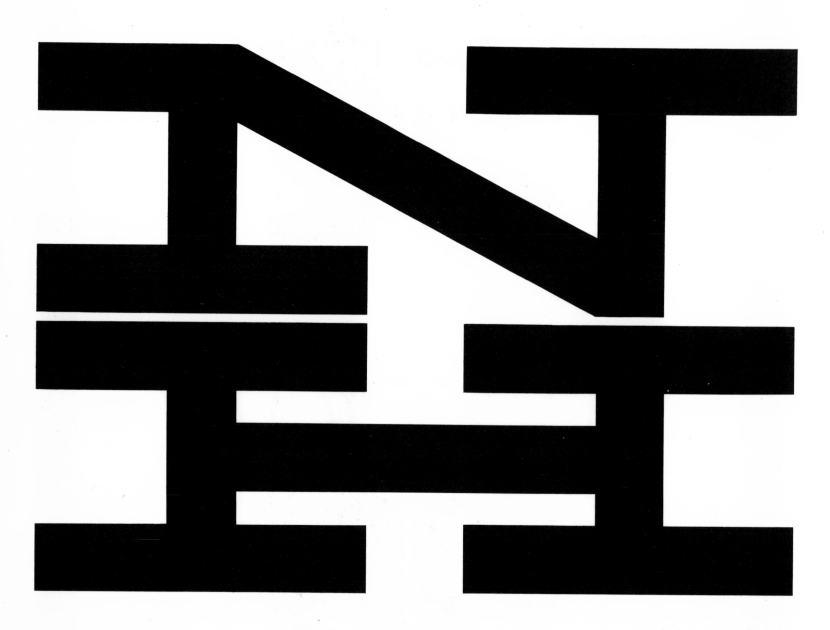

754

755

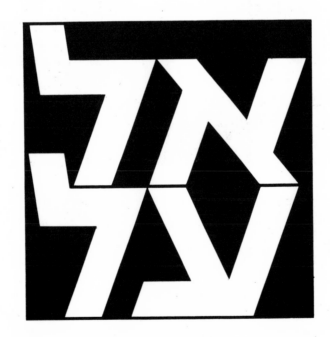

756

757

759

758

760

761

762

763

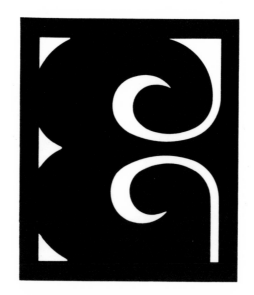

SOME NOTES ON TRADEMARK DESIGN

1

Practically all books published on trademarks start by describing their origin and history, then go on to provide examples classified according to one system or another, and end by discussing their use and effectiveness. Valid though this scheme may be, I have no intention of following it here.

I have prepared this book for designers and also for executives of companies and organizations who are responsible for selecting marks and symbols. It is possible that these executives may be more strongly impressed than designers by the unexpected world of symbols opening up before them in this book. Most people generally see trademarks or symbols standing alone and tend to think of them as unattractive, utilitarian things. In this book these isolated designs come together, at times seeming to interact like friends, or to complement one another, or to strike dramatic poses in unison.

It is the richness of themes and variations, and the lively vitality of the world of trademarks and symbols that I have attempted to show here—not only to designers and executives who commission symbols for their firms—but also to the general public to which the marks and symbols are directed.

It is common knowledge that in communicating with the public today, the mark or symbol makes an initial and important contribution. The corporate image starts with the mark, just as the laying of rails must be completed before the first train can run. Yet in regard to the trademarks, too many firms do not build upon the sound foundation needed to advance a favorable image.

Trademarks are an important means of guaranteeing product quality and of conveying the field of activity and scale of an enterprise. This is a fundamental principle in the creation of a corporate image.

"It is easier to remember a person's face than his name" is a statement often made in explaining the efficacy of trademarks. Most people do not pay attention outside their own sphere. How to impress a desirable image on this vast, indifferent public is a focal problem in present-day communications techniques.

In comparing the new trademarks and symbols sent to me from all over the world for this book with those in my earlier *Trademarks of the World* (New York, 1956), I must conclude that there has been no conspicuous progress in the intervening years. However, this is not surprising.

Trademarks and symbols always stretch the talent and capabilities of the designer to the utmost. Their creation involves a meeting at an extreme point of form and content. The conceptual ability of human beings to create such highly refined forms simply cannot be expected to show any major change in the span of ten years. Moreover, a long life span is demanded of trademarks and symbols. It would not do for them to look old-fashioned soon after they have been designed; they would then be more like vignettes for a weekly magazine rather than effective aids in creating an image of a firm or organization. Since a long life span is thus a basic prerequisite for a successful trademark, it should be no cause for concern that there are no basic differences in design concepts between this book and my previous one.

Yet this does not mean that there was no need to bring out this volume. As I mentioned previously, this book is an expression of my own feeling for design; it also represents a record of ten years as seen through marks and symbols. The compilation of an adequate record of the past is an essential step in the birth of something new.

In considering this book as a record of the past, the birth of a large number of new trademarks and symbols during these last ten years strikes me as a socio-economic phenomenon of considerable interest. It reflects the birth, or at least the rejuvenation, of a large number of firms and organizations. It is a phenomenon of much greater significance than the designing of huge quantities of posters and pamphlets; and mirrors what appears to be a much faster rate of change during this period than during the pre-war era. In compiling this volume, my attention has been drawn to a number of factors affecting this: a fierce economic competition; a great mass of new consumers who are quickly sated and always seeking new stimulants; a society ever more attuned to living in the present only, to stressing appearance more than content.

2

In *Seven Designers Look at Trademark Design* (published by Paul Theobald, 1952), there is an essay by Bernard Rudofsky entitled "Notes on Early Trademarks and Related Matters." It is the best discussion of the history of trademarks, and all later writings on this subject rely to a greater or lesser extent on this essay. It is perhaps unavoidable that most of the later works borrow only the historical, illustrative matter, and lack Rudofsky's great powers of philosophical insight. As I mentioned at the beginning, I see no need to discuss the history of trademarks here; I can do no better than to refer the reader to Rudofsky's essay on this subject.

However, I would like to call attention to the appearance of color in trademarks and symbols; this is a recent phenomenon. In principle, trademarks must be able to stand up

ALCOA's old mark. Red over blue.

to reproduction solely in black and white, because of the economics of mass-production printing. On the other hand, there is no doubt that the addition of color to trademarks and symbols greatly enhances their power to attract attention. The concept of the corporate image demands not only expression in a unique form but also its definite association with one particular color or combination of colors. One firm wants to express its "personality" through a blue-red combination; another chooses green for its color motif, and wants all its trucks painted green. The addition of color to trademarks raises difficult economic problems, but its effectiveness and strong appeal cannot be denied. A good example is the General Dynamics mark designed by Eric Nitsche (see page 66, No. 120). Between the letters G and D, eight different colors are inserted. This color scheme is used on letterheads and all other business forms. This mark raises various questions; from an economical point of view, it may be argued that it constitutes an unnecessary expense. However, from a design point of view, it can be maintained that this is an ideal way of creating an image. Perhaps it can be said that the adoption of the designer's ideas was made possible only because a design-oriented firm like General Dynamics was involved. In any event, the design is a bold, handsome one with a powerful appeal.

Saul Bass is the creator of the new mark of the Aluminum Corporation of America (ALCOA; see page 180, No. 497), which uses a combination of blue and red. Unfortunately, in this book it was impossible to reproduce it in the desired colors, and it is printed in green and black. ALCOA's old mark, in use before Saul Bass designed the new one, was also expressed in blue and red. In other words, this blue-red color scheme, with a triangle as its theme, was the basic symbol of the firm. In creating the new mark, Saul Bass succeeded in breathing fresh, pulsating life into this basic design of ALCOA. It takes a designer with a highly developed social sense to accomplish this.

I am one of those designers who do not place much faith in color theories. I believe that just about the only objects in which color problems can be solved successfully on the basis of theory are traffic signs. Colors with originality and fresh, artistic qualities are outside the province of theory. They are the result of delicate waves of sensibility within a single human being. It is the intuitive color sense of an artist, seeking to find an expression of his genius, which moves us. Many years ago, when I was young and foolish, I tried to do color analyses of the pictures of Paul Klee. I painted the individual colors one by one on 20-centimeter paper squares, but Paul Klee was nowhere to be found. There were only blue, or red, or yellow squares of paper. I tried to force Klee's colors into a combination in my designs, but the sensual, yet fresh and airy impression of his pictures, was entirely missing.

The matter may be dismissed by describing my efforts as childish, yet something close to what I did is being taught by color theorists. I have mentioned this because if the color shades used in trademarks are too subtle, they present difficulties in reproduction. Multi-color printing has made great strides, and so has the reproduction of color photographs, through advances in both photographic materials and printing techniques. As a result, trademarks are often reproduced in color along with color illustrations in advertisements. However, trademarks just as colorful as the pictures in the advertisements will recede into inconspicuousness, a phenomenon known to all concerned with design and printing. The common sense solution is the frequent use of simple and clear two-color combinations, such as red and black, black and green, black and yellow. It may be argued that, if this is so, there is no need for the intuitive color sense of a gifted artist, and that elementary color theory will be sufficient. This might be so if the only thing involved was the lining up of small squares of colored paper horizontally or vertically. Hewever, trademark design is the creation of forms of every conceivable shape. The proper matching of colors to these intricate forms calls for much more than mechanical application of color theory, and requires the talents of a gifted designer. There is a world of difference between the effect made by the right, "live" combination of two colors and a wrong, "dead" combination. Unless the two-color combination is dramatic, and forcefully strikes the viewer, it would be better to have the trademark or symbol in simple black and white.

Apart from the trademarks of commercial firms and the symbols of various organizations,

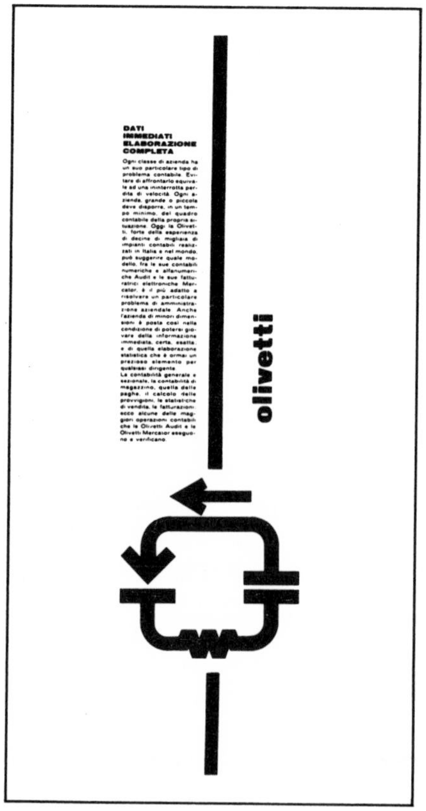

Examples of Olivetti advertisement applying symbols.

this book contains examples of what we might call signs or symbols used in advertising and product selling, such as the signs created by Giovanni Pintori for Olivetti products (Nos. 17, 33, 121, 137, 138, 139). They serve to impress upon the viewer the various calculating machines, typewriters, and other products produced by Olivetti, and are formed by the use of many colors. They play a star role in magazine advertisements and posters, and it is no exaggeration to say that they successfuly convey Olivetti's corporate image to the public. They are made up of clear, sharp colors. In this rare case, it might be said that the usual order of things has been reversed and that the individual gifts of the artist Pintori have shaped the characteristics of the Olivetti firm.

We see nothing strange in finger-prints being reproduced in black. But if those finger-prints are reproduced in red, they seem to reek of blood, and conjure up a scene of murder. Conversely, if a woman's lips are reproduced in black, it makes an eerie impression. We often hear of a woman sending her lover a letter ending with the red imprint of her lips. This is likely to stimulate the receiver sexually. But there are many different kinds of red. There is a sweet, romantic red, a dramatic, sexually exciting red, and others. It is said that the shape of every woman's lips is different, just as each person's finger-prints are unique. A woman's lips may thus be likened to her trademark, but the choice of lipstick color often expresses her character and breeding. The role of color in the corporate image is perhaps not unlike that of a woman's lipstick.

3

In my earlier book *Trademarks of the World*, I wrote:

"After a trademark has been selected, it must be tended. It must be kept fresh and alive. However, most businessmen become sentimentally attached to their marks and are reluctant to change that which has seen them through many hardships as well as success. If these men stubbornly stick to the old and are unwilling to modify and modernize, their beloved symbols will no longer appeal to the public."

Ten years later, these words have not lost their validity; there are still many unenlightened entrepreneurs who try to run a streamlined train, namely their modernized production facilities, on the outworn rails of an old trademark. Admittedly, changing a trademark requires courage; it involves altering what has been promoted at great cost for many years. But the one who generally thinks that the expense has been worthwhile is the entrepreneur. I believe that trademarks require periodic hormone injections—that they should be changed little by little, in inconspicuous ways—to bring them into line with the taste of the period while still maintaining their excellence, and giving the general public a feeling of continuity.

An outstandingly successful example of this is the case of the Westinghouse trademark designed by Paul Rand. If the old mark and the present mark are compared, there is definite continuity in image, while the freshness of the new mark seems to be a revelation of the progressive character of the company. It deserves special mention that Westinghouse also had a new logotype designed at the same time as the company changed its mark. The success of Westinghouse in this area is the joint product of the talents of a great designer

Former mark.

Distinguishing features of the Westinghouse logotype; the ligature "st" and "g".

and the wisdom and decisiveness of the company's executives.

About three years ago I was consulted by a middle ranking Japanese pharmaceutical manufacturer about a change of trademark. This firm had used a "P" in a circle for about 80 years, and was interested in rejuvenating this mark. A competition for a new mark was held among four of Japan's representative designers. With the finished marks before us, I explained to the president of the company that there were two ways of effecting a change in a trademark—a radical change, and a gradual change, one step at a time. The first way meant doing away with the old mark completely without leaving a trace of its image, thus giving the impression that a new firm had come into existence. If the second method was followed, people other than specialists would scarcely notice the change, yet a vague impression

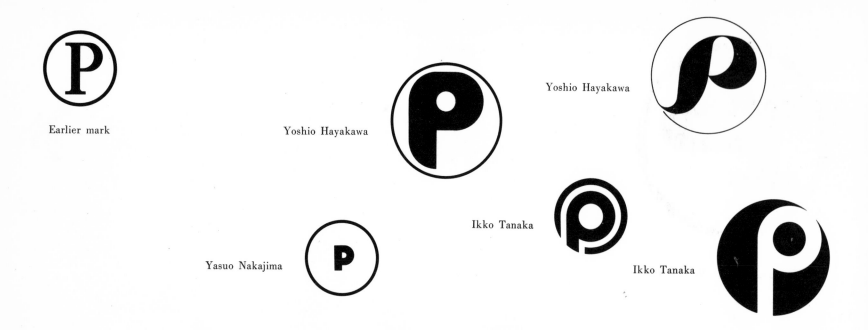

Earlier mark

Yoshio Hayakawa

Yoshio Hayakawa

Ikko Tanaka

Yasuo Nakajima

Ikko Tanaka

of rejuvenation would be conveyed. If the method of radical change was adopted everything else, such as newspaper advertisements, billboards, neon signs, and packages, would promptly have to be brought in line. This would involve enormous expense. With a one-step-at-a-time change, the process could be spread over a much longer period of time. The mark on boxes, for instance, could be changed when existing stocks were exhausted and a new printing ordered; billboards could be redesigned when physical replacement was necessary. I explained that the whole switch-over would take about two years and that it, of course, would cost much less than a radical change. In the end, the company decided to follow the one-step-at-a-time method.

I also pointed out it would be a mistake to think that the image of the company would become rejuvenated immediately just because of the new trademark. At the same time a new design policy would also have to be devised. So we also created a new logotype, and decided on a basic packaging design, in which, of course, the new trademark played a prominent part.

This case history is just one example from Japan; yet it shows the importance of using what may be called nothing more than ordinary common sense. Unfortunately this common

Selected new mark by Hiromu Hara

sense method is very seldom put into practice. Judging by my own experience, a company frequently commissions a new trademark from a designer, adopts it, and immediately feels that a distinct invigoration has taken place. But thereafter it does nothing to use the new trademark in a constructive and creative manner. No matter how much one may explain to the company executives what has to be done to utilize the new trademark fully, they do not listen. There are very few cases in which a company combines a new trademark with a new overall design policy, and thus really achieves successful results.

Outstanding examples of overall design planning are furnished by the works of Paul Rand for IBM (pages 22/23, Nos. 15, 16) and for Westinghouse (pages 120/121, Nos. 279, 280). The first step in drawing up an overall design policy is the creation of the trademark and of the logotype. Paul Rand's trademarks and logotypes (page 189, No. 560) possess a strength and beauty which transcend time, and thus have a very long life. They also have something which can be called "breadth." By this I mean that his marks fit in on any occasion and in any place. There are many interesting and appealing trademark designs: they may be chic, funny, light-hearted, or dramatic marks using new forms. However, their lack of breadth often becomes a problem. In other words, they are interesting and appealing but difficult to use.

They may not stand out when used on buildings; it may be impossible to make them into neon signs; they may not look good from a distance. Such marks all have the fault that only their original designers can use them to advantage. But marks and symbols must have sufficent breadth so that they come to life, whoever uses them. To come to life means that the mark or symbol does not interfere with other elements, but possesses the strength and beauty to harmonize with any surroundings.

4

A trademark or symbol must tell something about the purpose of the firm or organization it represents. This is a most elementary point to make about creating a corporate image, but one that cannot be overlooked. For example, it simply would not do if the marks of a chocolate manufacturer, a manufacturer of electrical appliances, and a steel works all conveyed a similar impression. In the mark of a chocolate manufacturer we want something of the sweetness and showiness of his products, while for a steel works mark we want an impression of weight and strength. It is not surprising that many airline marks take the form of birds, wings, or spears—conveying the impression of flight. Among the airlines of the world, nine use birds, four use wings, and another four use spears. This clearly shows the intention of the designers to strive for a simplified and yet easily recognizable image.

When I visited Max Huber's studio in Milan in 1964, I noticed that he was creating a strange, somehow unstable, half circle, with the letters "Besana" skilfully and dramatically placed at the bottom. I was interested in this unstable form and asked him about it. He explained that this was the form of a candy with the name imprinted on it—that was known to practically every Italian. The silhouette of the candy was being combined with the letters to make a very powerful trademark, to be put on everything, from wrapping paper to packages and trucks. This is an example of a successful overall design policy followed by a medium-size enterprise.

Another example of an easily understood and well thought-out trademark is that of the modular furniture manufacturer Christian Holzäpfel K.G. (pages 232/233, Nos. 751, 752) in Basel, designed by Karl Gerstner in collaboration with Gredinger & Kutter. This mark explains the concept of modular furniture brilliantly in very simple form. The letter "H" is designed in such a way as to give the impression of being an assembled unit; interestingly, it can be used side-ways either long and narrow, or short and squat. These variations in no way damage the image of the trademark. When it is used in magazine advertisements

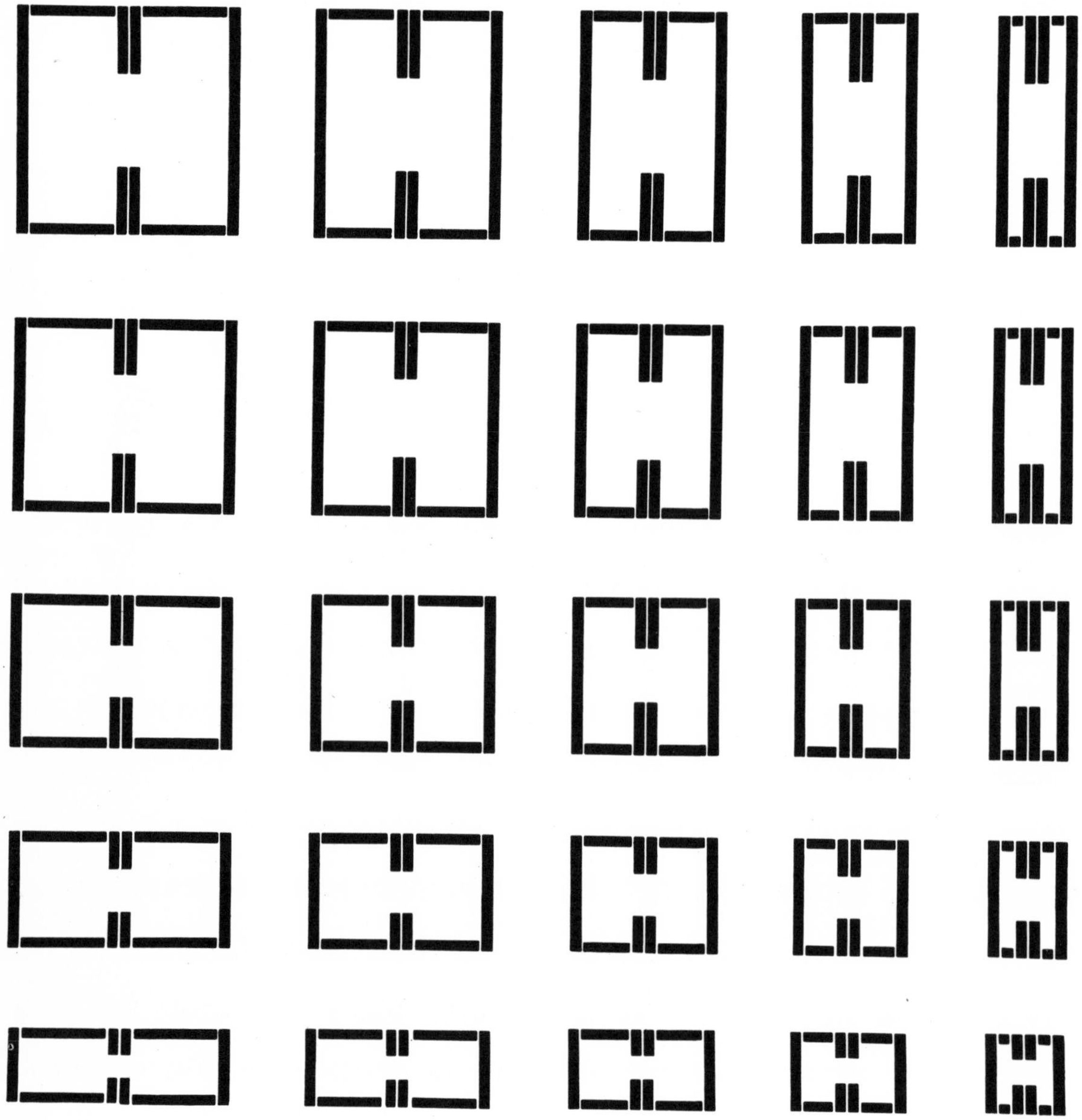

Variations of Holzäpfel trademark.

and pamphlets, the size of the mark is freely altered; however changed, it makes a strong impression on the viewer.

The trademark's function of clearly indicating the purpose of the enterprise is an important aid in sales. At the same time, it is highly desirable that the mark should also tell something about the size and nature of the enterprise for which it stands. It would not be appropriate for the marks of a one-man design office and a huge steel works, whose activity effects the economy of a whole country, to employ the same expression. Similarly, the trademark of a small store or workshop should not convey the same kind of impression as that of a huge electrical goods manufacturer. The mark should somehow express the scale and history of the enterprise, though this does not mean that it should have an antique air. What is neccessary is a suitable dignity.

Now let us assume that a good trademark has been chosen, and adopted by a company. The design is one that will make a strong, pleasant impression, and undoubtedly attract people. Unfortunately, such marks all too frequently end up in the president's desk drawer, or in the office safe, or only on stock certificates. A trademark exists to stamp itself indelibly upon the consciousness of the general public. This is the purpose of the corporate image. It must not be forgotten that a trademark has a strong psychological effect upon the general public. The image of a firm as huge, or outstanding, or progressive, or reliable owes much to the quality of the trademark design. Of course, the trademark by itself cannot create an image. Only where good design and overall design policy are combined, can a tiny mark in a corner of the product strongly convey the many facets of an image to the general public. Whether a trademark lives or dies depends on a careful and well thought-out design policy. Only if this exists, is it possible to deeply impress a corporate image on the general public.

ILLUSTRATION CREDITS

Note: Project indicates a design not in use at time of publication of this book.

11 1 Olle Eksell ⟨Sweden⟩ *Mazetti.* Chocolate manufacturer.

12 2 Anton Stankowski ⟨Germany⟩ *Standard Elektrik Lorenz AG.* Communications systems manufacturer.

13 3 George Giusti ⟨USA⟩ *Geigy.* Chemical and pharmaceutical manufacturer. Symbol for Hygroton.

14 4 Herb Lubalin, Inc. ⟨USA⟩ *Sudler, Hennessey & Lubalin.* Design division of Sudler & Hennessey, Inc., advertising agency.

15 5 Saul Bass ⟨USA⟩ *Eastman Kodak Pavilion, New York World's Fair '64-'65.* The searching eye.

6 Saul Bass ⟨USA⟩ *W.P. Fuller & Co.* Paint manufacturer.

16 7 Charles Loupot ⟨France⟩ *Airline.* (Project)

17 8 Morton Goldsholl Design Assoc. ⟨USA⟩ (Project)

18 9 Enzo Mari ⟨Italy⟩ *Danese.* Ceramic and porcelain products manufacturer. Package.

10 Franco Meneguzzo ⟨Italy⟩ *Danese.* Ceramic and porcelain products manufacturer.

19 11 Saul Bass ⟨USA⟩ *Lightcraft of California.* Lighting fixtures manufacturer.

20 12 Sy Edelstein ⟨USA⟩ *King Solomon.* Restaurant.

21 13 Robert R. Overby ⟨USA⟩ *Mitchell Travel Service.* Travel agents.

14 Rudolph de Harak ⟨USA⟩ *Ballard, Todd & Snibbe.* Architects.

22 15-16 Paul Rand ⟨USA⟩ *International Business Machines Corp.* Business machines manufacturer. Packages and logotype.

24 17 Giovanni Pintori ⟨Italy⟩ *Olivetti.* Symbol for Olivetti 48 typewriter.

25 18 Franco Grignani ⟨Italy⟩ *Maestrelli.* Textile studies center.

19 Max Huber ⟨Italy⟩ *Albitex.* Cotton mill.

26 20 Richard Shiffer / George Nelson & Co., Inc. ⟨USA⟩ *Rek-o-Kut.* Audio equipment manufacturer.

21 Collis Clements / Design Research Unit ⟨Great Britain⟩ *George Davidson & Co., Ltd.* Glass manufacturer.

22 Yusaku Kamekura ⟨Japan⟩ *Taiyo Machine Industry Co.* Machine tools manufacturer.

23 Ernst Roch ⟨Canada⟩ *Simtec Ltd.* Nuclear radiation detectors and monitors manufacturer.

27 24 Henrion Design Associates ⟨Great Britain⟩ *Brooks Ventilation Ltd.* Ventilation systems manufacturer.

28 25 Iris & Bruno Pippa ⟨Italy⟩ *Confezioni Coo.* Retail clothing store.

26 Heinz Waibl ⟨Italy⟩ *Franco Ranchetti S.p.A.* Photocopying equipment manufacturer.

27 Carl B. Graf ⟨Switzerland⟩ *Girsberger GmbH.* Furniture manufacturer.

28 Nedo Mien Ferrario ⟨Venezuela⟩ *Galeria Esniral.* Art gallery.

29 Allen, Dorsey & Hatfield ⟨USA⟩ *La Deau Manufacturing Co.* Symbol for Turnover Cradle, steel storage machine.

30 Jerry Berman Associates ⟨USA⟩ *Nadisco Inc.* Tire inflator distributor.

31 Anton Stankowski ⟨Germany⟩ Reproduction machinery manufacturer. (Project)

29 32 G. Soland + H. Schatzmann ⟨Switzerland⟩ *SAFFA.* Swiss exhibition of women's activities.

33 Giovanni Pintori ⟨Italy⟩ *Olivetti.* Business machines manufacturer.

30 34 Saul Bass ⟨USA⟩ "*Exodus.*" Motion picture.

31 35 Morton Goldsholl Design Associates ⟨USA⟩ *Butler Brothers.* Variety store chain. Private brands symbol.

36 Saul Bass ⟨USA⟩ *SANE.* Committee for a Sane Nuclear Policy.

32 37 Rudolph de Harak ⟨USA⟩ *National Association* of *Radio & TV Broadcasters.* Trade association.

38 Peter Graef ⟨USA⟩ *Castle & Cooke, Inc.* Food canners.

33 39 Gerd Leufert ⟨Venezuela⟩ *Venezuelan Pavillion, New York World's Fair '64-'65.*

34 40 Percy Wenger ⟨Switzerland⟩ *Schweizerische Verpackungs Prämierung.* Swiss competition of packaging designs.

35 41 Frank Wagner ⟨USA⟩ *CBS Radio Network.* Symbol for a radio program.

36 42 Max Huber ⟨Italy⟩ *NAVA.* Printing company.

43 Fred Witig / George Nelson & Co., Inc. ⟨USA⟩ *Structural Products Inc.* Aluminum products manufacturer.

44 Wim Crouwel ⟨Netherlands⟩ *Nederlandse Kunsttichting.* Arts federation.

45 Yusaku Kamekura ⟨Japan⟩ *Japan Photographers Society.*

46 Lester Beall, Inc. ⟨USA⟩ *Merrill Lynch, Pierce, Fenner & Smith, Inc.* Stock brokers.

37 47-48 Paul Rand ⟨USA⟩ *Harcourt Brace & World, Inc.* Book publishers.

38 49 Max Huber ⟨Italy⟩ *22 Dicembre.* Movie productions.

50 F.H.K. Henrion ⟨Great Britain⟩ *Layton Awards.* Competition for printing techniques.

51 Bob Noorda ⟨Italy⟩. *La Rinascente / UPIM.* Department store chain. Quality control symbol.

52 Max Huber ⟨Italy⟩ *Temi S.p.A.* Newspaper publisher and printer.

39 53 Max Huber ⟨Italy⟩ *Coin.* Department stores.

54 Albe Steiner ⟨Italy⟩ *Foto Studio 22.* Photographers.

40 55 Hans Neuburg ⟨Switzerland⟩ *Plüss.* Printing company.

56 G. Soland ⟨Switzerland⟩ *Union of Swiss Consumers Associations.* Co-operative food stores.

57 Alfred Willimann ⟨Switzerland⟩ *Lignoplast A.G.* Interior decorators.

58 Alfred Willimann ⟨Switzerland⟩ *Gromalto A.G.* Paint manufacturers.

41 59-61 Kurt Wirth ⟨Switzerland⟩ *Buri & Cie.* Printers.

42 62-64 Paul Rand ⟨USA⟩ *Atlas Crankshaft Corp.* Crankshafts manufacturer.

44 65 M. Schneider/Studio Boggeri <Italy> *Cantoni S.p.A.* Textile manufacturer.

66 Motoi Shigenari ⟨Japan⟩ *Toyobo Textile Co.* Showroom symbol.

45 67 Eckstein-Stone, Inc. ⟨USA⟩ *Dusal instrument.* Scientific instruments manufacturer.

68 Brownjohn & Chermayeff & Geismar ⟨USA⟩ *Malacandra Productions.* High fidelity recording firm.

69 Hans Schleger ⟨Great Britain⟩ *Design Center.* Housemark.

70 Rolf Harder ⟨Canada⟩ Venetian blinds manufacturer. (Project)

46 71 Push Pin Studios, Inc. ⟨USA⟩ *L'Escargot D'Or.* Restaurant.

72 Morton Goldsholl Design Associates ⟨USA⟩ *Storkline Furniture.* Baby furniture manufacturer.

47 73 Erberto Carboni ⟨Italy⟩ *Ceramiques Laveno.* Ceramics manufacturer.

74 Yusaku Kamekura ⟨Japan⟩ *Aburatsubo Yacht Club.*

75 Arthur Paul ⟨USA⟩ *Playboy International.* Publisher, restaurateur, hotelier.

48 76 Neil Fujita ⟨USA⟩ *Record Source, Inc.* Publication.

77 Appelbaum & Curtis ⟨USA⟩ *Richmond Research Corp.* Picture projectors manufacturer.

78 Robert R. Overby ⟨USA⟩ *Mel Whitson Stationers, Inc.* Stationers.

49 79 Studio Boggeri ⟨Italy⟩ *Cantoni S.p.A.* Textile manufacturer.

80 Klaus Winterhäger ⟨Germany⟩ C. *Feldmann.* Woodworking tools manufacturer.

49 81 Benno Wissing ⟨Netherlands⟩ *Aviso N.V.S.A.* Building materials importer and wholesaler.

82 F.H.K. Henrion ⟨Great Britain⟩ *Square Grip Reinforcement Co., Ltd.* Reinforcing steel manufacturer.

50 83 Walter Allner ⟨USA⟩ *Fortune Films.* Film producers.

51 84 Lippincott & Margulies, Inc. ⟨USA⟩ *United Van Lines, Inc.* Transporters.

85 Makoto Wada ⟨Japan⟩ *Mainichi Newspapers.* Advertising design contest symbol.

86 Walter Bosshardt ⟨Switzerland⟩ *Werner Noll.* Optician.

87 Morton Goldsholl Design Associates ⟨USA⟩ Advertising agency. (Project)

52 88 Ernst Roch ⟨Canada⟩ *Montreal International Fair.*

89 M. Schneider/Studio Boggeri <Italy> *Cantoni S.p.A.* Textile manufacturer.

53 90 Neil Fujita ⟨USA⟩ *Worldwide Broadcasting Company.* Radio broadcasters.

91 Erik Nitsche ⟨USA⟩ *Dorland, Inc.* Advertising agency.

54 92 Everett S. Aison ⟨USA⟩ Film Pathways, Inc. Motion picture producers.

93 Leo Monahan ⟨USA⟩ *Eden Records.* Popular records producer.

55 94 Saul Bass ⟨USA⟩ "*Anatomy of A Murder.*" Motion picture.

56 95 Morton Goldsholl Design Associates ⟨USA⟩ *Munising Paper Co.* Printing and typewriter paper manufacturer.

96 Albe Steiner ⟨Italy⟩ *Libra.* Book store.

57 97 Robert Geiber ⟨Switzerland⟩ *Krefina Bank A.G.* Bank.

98 Morton Goldsholl Design Associates ⟨USA⟩ *Peace Corps.*

58 99 Otl Aicher and Tomas Gonda ⟨Germany⟩ Oil trade company. (Project)

100-101 Herbert Leupin ⟨Switzerland⟩ *Andre.* Men's clothing store.

59 102 Ernst Roch ⟨Canada⟩ *Haas.* Rope manufacturers.

103 Peter Ray ⟨Great Britain⟩ *The Turks Head.* Pub.

60 104 Push Pin Studios Inc. ⟨USA⟩ Own symbol. Graphic designers.

105 Hermann Eidenbenz ⟨Switzerland⟩ *Papyrus A.G.* Stationers.

106 Giulio Confalonieri ⟨Italy⟩ *Ditta Vergottini.*

61 107 Herb Lubalin Inc. ⟨USA⟩ Opening announcement of own design firm.

62 108 Theo Dimson ⟨Canada⟩ *Marlborough Hotel.*

109 Herb Lubalin Inc. ⟨USA⟩ *Sand Grenade.* Product for snow driving.

63 110 Theo Dimson ⟨Canada⟩ Printed matter for 12th Annual Award Ceremony of *Art Directors Club, Toronto.*

64 111 Max Bill ⟨Switzerland⟩ *Wohnbedarf A.G.* Homefurnishing manufacturer and retailer.

112 Alfred Willimann ⟨Switzerland⟩ *Karl Steiner.* Carpenters.

113 G. Soland ⟨Switzerland⟩ *Pendt A.G.* Shop builders.

114 Noel Martin ⟨USA⟩ *Westab.* Stationers and school supply manufacturer.

65 115 Heinz Waibl ⟨Italy⟩ *Allumino S.p.A.* Aluminum corporation.

116 Pierre Gauchat ⟨Switzerland⟩ *Riri Werke.* Zip fastener manufacturer.

117 Carlo Vivarelli ⟨Switzerland⟩ *Therma A.G.* Electrical appliances manufacturer.

118 Albe Steiner ⟨Italy⟩ *Ar-flex S.p.A.* Upholstered furniture manufacturer.

66 119 Don Ervin / George Nelson & Co., Inc. ⟨USA⟩ American National Exhibition in Moscow.

120 Erik Nitsche ⟨USA⟩ *General Dynamics Corp.* Defense systems manufacturer.

67 121 Giovanni Pintori ⟨Italy⟩ *Olivetti.* Business machines manufacturer. closed.

68 122 Hans Neuburg ⟨Switzerland⟩ *Hyspa 1961.* Hygiene and sport exhibition. rotation + vitality function as sign

123 Robert Sanbonet ⟨Italy⟩ *Triennale.* Design exhibition.

124 Carl B. Graf ⟨Switzerland⟩ *Kurth Certina Frères S.A.* Watch makers.

125 Kurt Wirth ⟨Switzerland⟩ *Chemische Fabrik Aarberg.* Printing colors manufacturer.

69 126 Kurt Wirth ⟨Switzerland⟩ *Swiss National Exhibition 1964.*

127 Lester Beall, Inc. ⟨USA⟩ *The Bunker-Ramo Corp.* Computer systems manufacturer.

128 Takashi Kono ⟨Japan⟩ *World Design Conference, Tokyo.* INITIALS → SYMBOLS VISUALLY ORGANIZED

129 Gustavo Balcells ⟨Argentina⟩ *Allende & Brea.* Patent agent.

130 Push Pin Studios, Inc. ⟨USA⟩ *Little, Brown & Co.* Book publishers.

131 Ove Engström ⟨Sweden⟩ *Bröderna Larsson.* Men's clothing manufacturer.

132 Alejandro Moy ⟨Argentina⟩ *The Argentine Chamber of Realtors.*

133 Otl Aicher ⟨Germany⟩ *Stuttgarter Gardinenfabrik.* Textile manufacturer.

134 A. Paez Torres ⟨Argentina⟩ *Fundacion Empresaizia.* Executives club.

135 Ernst Roch ⟨Canada⟩ *George F. Eber.* Architect.

136 Ernst Roch ⟨Canada⟩ *Artwood.* Office furniture manufacturer.

70 137-139 Giovanni Pintori ⟨Italy⟩ *Olivetti.* Symbol for electric computor.

71 140-141 Ladislav Sutnar ⟨USA⟩ *Carr's.* Department store.

72 142 Saul Bass ⟨USA⟩ *"The Cardinal."* Motion picture.

73 143 Morton Goldsholl Design Associates ⟨USA⟩ *International Minerals & Chemicals Corp.* Mineral and chemical manufacturer.

144 Chris Yaneff + Manfred Gotthans ⟨Canada⟩ *United Dominions Corp.* Finance company.

74 145 Cecco Re ⟨Italy⟩ *A & B Insurance Brokers.*

146 Cecco Re ⟨Italy⟩ *Impresi Turistiche Barziesi.* Tourist organization.

75 147 Heinz Waibl ⟨Italy⟩ *Termica.* Air conditioning machinery manufacturer.

148 Heinz Waibl ⟨Italy⟩ *Pagina.* Graphic design magazine.

149 Cecco Re ⟨Italy⟩ *Collana discografica IBC.* Record series.

76 150 Cecco Re ⟨Italy⟩ *Collana discografica IBC.* Record series.

151 Gianni Venturino ⟨Italy⟩ *Calzificio Re Depaolini.* Hosiery store.

152 Walter Ballmer ⟨Italy⟩ *Societa Italo Svizzera Fusioni Inettate.*

153 Freeman Craw ⟨USA⟩ *CA.* Journal of commercial art.

154 Lester Beall, Inc. ⟨USA⟩ *Martin Marietta Corp.* Electronic and nuclear manufacturers.

155 Anton Stankowski ⟨Germany⟩ *Spinner.* Department store.

77 156 Takashi Kono ⟨Japan⟩ *Aji-no-moto.* Seasoning manufacturer.

157 Takashi Kono ⟨Japan⟩ *Tombow Pencil Manufacturing Co.* Pencil symbol.

158 Takashi Kono ⟨Japan⟩ *Miwa Pearl Co., Ltd.*

78 159 Karl Gerstner ⟨Switzerland⟩ *Arthur Niggli Verlag.* Book publisher.

160 Hans Neuburg ⟨Switzerland⟩ *Eggler & Itschner.* Machine manufacturer for the paint industry.

161 G. Honegger and G. Soland ⟨Switzerland⟩ *B.A.G. Turgi.* Lighting fixtures manufacturer.

162 Heinz Waibl ⟨Italy⟩ *ENEL.* Electric Power Corporation.

79 163 Armin Hofmann ⟨Switzerland⟩ *Swiss National Fair, Lausanne 1964.*

164 Noel Martin ⟨USA⟩ *Champion Paper Inc.* Paper manufacturer.

165 Masayoshi Nakajo ⟨Japan⟩ *Asama Motor Lodge.*

166 Keith Bright ⟨USA⟩ *Contact Products, Inc.* Pressure-sensitive paper manufacturer.

80 167 Ernst Roch ⟨Canada⟩ *Halifax Shopping Center.*

168 Rose-Marie Joray ⟨Switzerland⟩ *Gottfried Pfenninger.* Electrical appliances.

80 169 Kenneth R. Hollick <USA> *Amosco.* Amalgated Asphalt Co. Ltd.

170 F.H.K. Henrion <Great Britain> *Simplex Concrete Piles Ltd.* Pile drivers.

171 R. Nelson, W. Bartch & Associates <USA> *George W. Barton & Associates.* Highway and traffic consultants.

172 Martti A. Mykkänen <Finland> *Asfaltor Oy.* Road constructors.

173 Jun Tabohashi <Japan> *Dentsu Driving Club.*

174 Martti A. Mykkänen <Finland> *Jalo Haapala & Co.* Construction company.

175 Jacques Nathan-Garamond <France> *Les Créations Graphiques.* Printers.

176 Gerd Leufert <Venezuela> *Ximenez Hnos.* Exporters-importers.

177 R.W. Mutch & Co. <USA> *Pockman Manufacturing Co.* Poultry coop wire and ventilating systems manufacturer.

178 Jun Tabohashi <Japan> *Prince Motor Sales Co. Ltd.* Car symbol.

81 179 Jacques Nathan-Garamond <France> *OECD.* Organization for Economic Expansion.

82 180 Tomoko Miho / George Nelson & Co., Inc. <USA> *Everbrite.* Electric signs manufacturer.

181 Erberto Carboni <Italy> *Exhibition: Italian Regions.*

83 182 Morton Goldsholl Design Associates <USA> *Miles Laboratories, Inc.* Pharmaceutical manufacturer. Symbol for Bactine skin cream.

183 Yusaku Kamekura <Japan> *Japanese National Commitee for World Power Conference.*

184 Rudolph de Harak <USA> *Cumberland Furniture Corp.* Furniture manufacturer.

185 Yusaku Kamekura <Japan> *Kinyo.* Textile wholesalers.

186 Albe Steiner <Italy> *Camadis S.p.A.*

84 187 George Him <Great Britain> *Australian Trade Commission.* Identification for Australian Sunshine Foods.

188 L. Sturne <Italy> *La Rinascente / UPIM.* Department store chain. Ceramic seal.

189 Bob Noorda <Italy> *La Comete.* Advertising agency for film and TV publicity.

190 Masayoshi Nakajo <Japan> *Ginza Shashin-Kosha.* Photography studio.

191 Ernst Roch <Canada> *Creative Photographers, Inc.* Photographic studio.

192 Marcel Wyss <Switzerland> *Roland von Siebenthal.* Potographers.

193 Anton Stankowski <Germany> Constructors. (Project)

194 Anton Stankowski <Germany> Constructors. (Project)

85 195 Anton Stankowski <Germany> Television signet for diaphragm and tower. (Project)

86 196 Helmut Lortz <Germany> *College of Fine Arts, Berlin.*

86 197 Anton Stankowski ⟨Germany⟩ *Planen und Wohnen.* Furniture store.

198 Ernst Roch ⟨Canada⟩ *Montreal Chamber Orchestra.*

199 Anton Stankowski ⟨Germany⟩ *Kornhaus.* Textile company.

87 200 Yusaku Kamekura ⟨Japan⟩ *Kenchiku-ka Kyokai.* Architects Association.

88 201 Yusaku Kamekura ⟨Japan⟩ *Yuken-boeki.* Mail order house.

202 Yusaku Kamekura ⟨Japan⟩ *Cultural exchange association.* (Project)

203 Yusaku Kamekura ⟨Japan⟩ *Daishowa Seishi.* Paper mills.

89 204 Morton Goldsholl Design Associates ⟨USA⟩ Electronics Company. (Project)

205 Don Ervin / George Nelson & Co., Inc. ⟨USA⟩ *Abbott Co.* Pharmaceuticals manufacturer.

90 206 Morton Goldsholl Design Associates ⟨USA⟩ Electronics company. (Project)

207 Morton Goldsholl Design Associates ⟨USA⟩ *Bauer & Black.* Elastic health garments manufacturer.

208 Morton Goldsholl Design Associates ⟨USA⟩ Vibrator and appliances manufacturer. (Project)

91 209 Morton Goldsholl Design Associates ⟨USA⟩ *Spencer Stuart & Associates.* Management consultants.

92 210 Max Huber ⟨Italy⟩ *Habitat.* Builders.

211 George Tscherny ⟨USA⟩ *Robert Zeidman Associates, Inc.* Industrial and package designers.

212 Jacques Nathan-Garamond ⟨France⟩ *Society of Industrial Arts.*

213 Walter Allner ⟨USA⟩ *Tri Inc.* Advertising Agency.

93 214 Takeshi Otaka ⟨Japan⟩ *Nada-man.* Restaurant.

215 Takeshi Otaka ⟨Japan⟩ *Hanataba.* Night club.

216 Takeshi Otaka ⟨Japan⟩ *Hitotsubu.* Restaurant.

217 Klaus Winterhäger ⟨Germany⟩ *Hans Winterhager, VDI.* Engineering office.

218 Michele Provinciali ⟨Italy⟩ *Poretti S.p.A.* Brewers.

94 219 Herb Lubalin Inc. ⟨USA⟩ *Eros Magazine, Inc.* Publication.

220 Herb Lubalin Inc. ⟨USA⟩ *Liaison Newsletter, Inc.* Publication.

95 221-222 Theo Dimson ⟨Canada⟩ *Harridge's.* Women's clothing store.

96 223 Push Pin Studios, Inc. ⟨USA⟩ *Franklin Simon.* Department store chain.

97 224 Helmut Lortz ⟨Germany⟩ Own symbol.

225 Romulo Maccio ⟨Argentina⟩ *Mirasol Libros.* Book publishers.

98 226 Aldo Calabresi / Studio Boggeri ⟨Italy⟩ *Tesom.* Men's clothing manufacturer.

227 Shigeo Fukuda ⟨Japan⟩ *Toyoko Department Store.* Symbol for merchandise series.

99 228 Hans Neuburg ⟨Switzerland⟩ + Anton Stankowski ⟨Germany⟩ *Sulzer AG.* Heavy machinery manufacturer.

229 Max Huber / Studio Boggeri ⟨Italy⟩ *Vitam.* Dried fruit company.

100 230 George Giusti ⟨USA⟩ *Doubleday & Co.* Book publishers. Symbol for American history series.

101 231 Arnold Schwartzmann ⟨Great Britain⟩ *Creative Partners Ltd.* Script-writers.

232 June Fraser / Design Research Unit ⟨Great Britain⟩ *Hodder Publications, Ltd.* Book publishers.

233 Goerge Giusti ⟨USA⟩ *Doubleday & Co.* Book publishers. Dolphin books series.

102 234 Giulio Confalonieri ⟨Italy⟩ *St. Andrews.* Restaurant.

235 Giulio Confalonieri ⟨Italy⟩ *Glencannon Whisky.*

236 Giulio Confalonieri ⟨Italy⟩ *The Whisky House.* Italian-English import firm.

103 237 Milner Gray / Design Research Unit ⟨Great Britain⟩ *Watney, Combe, Reid & Co., Ltd.* Brewers.

238 Kenneth Lamble and Collis Clements / Design Research Unit ⟨Great Britain⟩ *Dunlop Footwear Ltd.* Rubber footwear manufacturer.

104 239 Ronald Armstrong / Design Research Unit ⟨Great Britain⟩ *International Distillers and Vintners, Ltd.*

105 240 Giulio Confalonieri ⟨Italy⟩ Italian-English importers. (Project)

241 Ronald Armstrong / Design Research Unit ⟨Great Britain⟩ *Buisiness Equipment Trade Association.*

242 H.A. Rothholz & Associates ⟨Great Britain⟩ *Winsor & Newton Ltd.* Art supplies manufacturer.

243 Erik Ellegaard Frederiksen ⟨Denmark⟩ *SIG.* Swedish Association of Poster Designers.

106 244 Marcel Jacno ⟨France⟩ *Alhambra.* Music-hall.

245 Marcel Jacno ⟨France⟩ *Théâtre National Populaire.*

246 Morton Goldsholl Design Associates ⟨USA⟩ *Foulds Co.* Pasta manufacturer.

107 247 Jacques Nathan-Garamond ⟨France⟩ *OECD.* Organization for Economic Expansion.

248 June Fraser / Design Research Unit ⟨Great Britain⟩ *Finlay Shields.* Linen and towelling manufacturer.

108 249 Marco Del Corno ⟨Italy⟩ *Organizzazione Scuolo Nord.* School Organization.

250 Lello Castellaneta ⟨Italy⟩ *Balatum Italiana.* Tile manufacturer.

251 Helmuth Kurtz ⟨Switzerland⟩ *Evangelischer Verband Frauenhilfe.* Religious organization.

252 Ernst Roch ⟨Canada⟩ *Man and His World.* Canadian World Exhibition Corporation.

253 Keiko Hirohashi ⟨Japan⟩ *Meiji-Seimei.* Life insurance company.

108 254 Ernst Roch <Canada> *William S. Merrell Co.* Pharmaceutical manufacturer.

109 255 Rolf Harder <Canada> *Canadian Association for Retarded Children.*

110 256 Ernst Roch <Canada> *Riverside Housing.* Building Contractor.

257 Yusaku Kamekura <Japan> *Nihon Prefab Jutaku.* Prefabricated housing manufacturer.

258 Ernst Roch <Canada> *Smith Construction Corporation.* Building Contractor.

259 Jean Picart Le Doux <France> *Fonderies de Pont-à-Mousson.* Foundries.

111 260 Milner Gray / Design Research Unit <Great Britain> *Building Center.*

261 Lester Beall Inc. <USA> *International Paper Co.* Paper manufacturer.

112 262 Giulio Confalonieri <Italy> *Ditta Lerici Editori.* Publishers.

113 263 Celestino Piatti <Switzerland> *Artemis Verlag.* Publisher.

114 264 Bob Noorda <Italy> *Vallecchi Editore.* Publishers.

265 Lars Bramberg <Sweden> *Nordiska Mässor.* Exhibition of Swedish cultural and industrial activities.

115 266-267 Lester Beall, Inc. <USA> *Hilton Hotel, New York.*

116 268 Saul Bass <USA> *Lawry's Food Products, Inc.* Spices and seasonings manufacturer.

269 Lester Beall, Inc. <USA> *Titeflex, Inc.* Flexible tubing manufacturer.

270 Saul Bass <USA> *Lawry's Food Products, Inc.* Spices and seasonings manufacturer.

117 271 Otl Aicher <Germany> *Steiger & Deschler.* Textile manufacturer.

272 Theo Dimson <Canada> *William R. Rundle Ltd.* Importers.

273 Bradbury Thompson <USA> *Society of Illustrators.*

274 Olle Eksell <Sweden> *Nils Nessim.* Carpet store.

118 275 Morton Goldsholl Design Associates <USA> *Munising Paper Co.* Paper manufacturer.

276 Eckstein-Stone, Inc. <USA> *H. &. K. Gross.* Textile manufacturer.

119 277 Morton Goldsholl Design Associates <USA> *Ditto Company, Inc.* Duplication products manufacturer. Package.

278 Morton Goldsholl Design Associates <USA> *Ditto Company Inc.* Duplication products manufacturer.

120 279-280 Paul Rand <USA> *Westinghouse.* Electrical products manufacturer.(photo: Y. Ishimoto)

122 281 Gerd Leufert <Venezuela> *Pierre Denis.* Antique shop.

123 282 Yusaku Kamekura <Japan> *Takasaka Country Club.*

124 283 Jerry Braude <USA> *Boles-Aero Travel Trailer.* Transport company.

124 284 Rolf Harder ⟨Canada⟩ (Project)

285 Rolf Harder ⟨Canada⟩ Chicken farm. (Project)

286 Jan Hollender ⟨Poland⟩ *Pronit.* Record company.

287 Jan Hollender ⟨Poland⟩ *Slendaire.* Plastic surgery clinic.

288 Jerzy Cherka ⟨Poland⟩ *Iskry.* Publisher.

125 289 Stefan Bernacinski ⟨Czechoslovakia⟩ *Nasza Ksiegarnia.* Publisher.

290 Toni Burghart ⟨Germany⟩ *Täuber & Sohn.* Publisher.

291 Jiří Rathouský ⟨Czechoslovakia⟩ *Czechoslovak Airlines.*

292 Jiří Rathouský ⟨Czechoslovakia⟩ Artist's signet.

293 Fritjof Pedersen ⟨Sweden⟩ *Bonving Skofabrik.* Men's shoes manufacturer.

294 Seymour Augenbraum ⟨USA⟩ *Sterling Forest Gardens.* Park.

126 295 Saul Bass ⟨USA⟩ *The Trane Company.** Ventilating systems manufacturer.

296 Saul Bass ⟨USA⟩ *Ivan Allen Company.** Office supply retailers.

297 Theo Dimson ⟨Canada⟩ *Green, Blankstein & Russell, Ltd.* Architects.

298 Erik Nitsche ⟨USA⟩ Own letterhead.

127 299 Saul Bass ⟨USA⟩ *Samsonite.** Luggage and folding furniture manufacturer. Luggage division.

300 Erik Nitsche ⟨USA⟩ *International Golf Association.*

301 George Tscherny ⟨USA⟩ *American Design Foundation.* Furniture manufacturer.

302 George Tscherny ⟨USA⟩ *Design Built Exhibits, Inc.* Exhibit and display builder.

128 303 Ralph Eckerstrom ⟨USA⟩ *Container Corporation of America.* Container manufacturer.

129 304 Kenji Ito ⟨Japan⟩ *Hotel Kirishima.*

305 Takashi Kono ⟨Japan⟩ *Daiwa Manekin Company.* Display models manufacturer.

130 306 Toshihiro Katayama ⟨Japan⟩ *Geigy.* Pharmaceutical manufacturer. Symbol for Hygroton.

307 George Giusti ⟨USA⟩ *Geigy.* Pharmaceutical manufacturer. Symbol for Preludin.

131 308 Saul Bass ⟨USA⟩ *Committee of Aluminum Producers.*

309 Matthew Leibowitz ⟨USA⟩ *Vector Manufacturing Co.* Electronic and aerospace instruments manufacturer.

132 310 Kurt Wirth ⟨Switzerland⟩ *Lithografie Zeiler AG.* Printer.

133 311 Giulio Confalonieri ⟨Italy⟩ *Ditta Lerici Editori.* Publisher.

*These are dummy letterheads (not in use) designed for a promotion booklet of sample letterheads for *Kimberly–Clark Corp.*, paper manufacturer.

134 312 Donald C. Smith ⟨USA⟩ *Art Directors & Designers' Association of New Orleans.*

313 Yusaku Kamekura ⟨Japan⟩ *Niigata-nippo.* Newspaper.

314 Augusto Concato ⟨Italy⟩ *Innocenti.* Automobile and machine manufacturer.

315 M. Schneider / Studio Boggeri <Italy> (Project)

135 316 Robert Berndt ⟨Germany⟩ Mail order house. (Project)

317 Lester Beall Inc. ⟨USA⟩ *Western Gypsum Products, Ltd.* Paint, plaster and cement manufacturer.

318 A. Ross and B. Thompson ⟨USA⟩ *Davis Delaney.* Printer.

136 319 Royal Dadman Associates ⟨USA⟩. *Diamond Alkali Co.* Chemical products manufacturer.

320 Gianni Venturino ⟨Italy⟩ *Rumianca S.p.A.* Chemical products manufacturer.

137 321 Paul Rand ⟨USA⟩ *United Parcel Service.* Parcel delivery company.

322 Pier Vico Cortesi ⟨Italy⟩ *Arti Grafiche Fantoni.* Graphic artists.

323 Wolfgang Freitag ⟨Germany⟩ Mail order house. (Project)

138 324 Ilio Negri ⟨Italy⟩ *Silkrom.*

325 Armin Hofmann ⟨Switzerland⟩ *Däniken.* Cable manufacturer.

326 Aldo Calabresi / Studio Boggeri ⟨Italy⟩ *Superga Industria Scarpe.* Shoe manufacturer.

327 Paul Rand ⟨USA⟩ *American Broadcasting Co.* Radio and TV network.

328 Ernst Roch ⟨Canada⟩ *Toilet Laundries Ltd.* Laundry and cleaning service.

329 Yusaku Kamekura ⟨Japan⟩ Japanese government seal of design approval.

330 Kohei Sugiura ⟨Japan⟩ *Tokyo Gallery.* Art gallery.

139 331 Albe Steiner ⟨Italy⟩ *Stagni.* Machinery manufacturer.

332 Hans Neuburg ⟨Switzerland⟩ *Ing. W. Oertli AG.* Oil heater manufacturer.

333 Jacques Richez ⟨Belgium⟩ *Brewery B.G.*

334 Jacques Richez ⟨Belgium⟩ *Atelier 3D.*

335 Allan R. Fleming + Jim Donahue ⟨Canada⟩ *Erin Mills Developments, Ltd.*

336 Judith Fralick ⟨Canada⟩ *MacDonald-Downie Ltd.* Printer

140 337 Jacques Nathan-Garamond ⟨France⟩ *Plastugyl.* Plastic manufacturer.

338 Ikko Tanaka ⟨Japan⟩ *Toyota Motor Co., Ltd.* Symbol for the Publica automobile.

339 Jiří Rathousky ⟨Czechoslovakia⟩ Record edition.

140 340 Enzo Rösli ⟨Switzerland⟩ *Zip.* Match factory.

341 Marcel Wyss ⟨Switzerland⟩ *Rolf Jenni.* Musical instrument manufacturer.

342 Raymond Loewy Associates ⟨France⟩ *Nobel Bozel.* Chemical company.

343 R. Manson + v. Zuffellato ⟨Italy⟩ *Tito Piccoli Fotografo.* Photographers.

344 Kenji Ito ⟨Japan⟩ *Daido Interior Co., Ltd.* Decorators.

141 345 Jacques Nathan-Garamond ⟨France⟩ *Les Créations Graphiques.* Publisher.

346 Primo Angeli ⟨USA⟩ *Eastman Associates.* Public relations.

347 Mitsuo Katsui ⟨Japan⟩ *Sunayama Productions.* TV commercial films.

348 Wim Crouwel ⟨Netherlands⟩ *Municipal Museum van Abbe, Eindhoven.*

349 Yusaku Kamekura ⟨Japan⟩ *Dainippon Printing Ink & Chemical Co., Ltd.*

350 Otto Brunner ⟨Germany⟩ *Armaturenfabrik und Metallgiesserei.*

142 351 Chuck Rhoades ⟨USA⟩ *Continental Savings & Loan.* Bank.

352 Anton Stankowski ⟨Germany⟩ *Lufttechnische Gesellschaft.* Airconditioning and heating manufacturer.

353 Nedo Mien Feriario ⟨Venezuela⟩ *Banco Hipotecario de Credito Unido.* Bank.

354 Romulo Maccio ⟨Italy⟩ *Ediciones Mundonuevo.* Publisher.

355 Franco Grignani ⟨Italy⟩ Committee for Silk in Italy.

143 356 Anton Stankowski ⟨Germany⟩ *Lufttechnische Gesellschaft.* Airconditioning and heating manufacturer.

357 Muriel Cooper ⟨USA⟩ *M.I.T. Press.* Publishers.

358 Jacques Richez ⟨Belgium⟩ *Estro Armonico.* Club.

359 Carlo Vivarelli ⟨Switzerland⟩ *JWS.* Building machinery manufacturer.

360 Ladislav Sutnar ⟨USA⟩ *M-M Enclosures, Inc.* Metal containers manufacturer.

144 361 Herbert Auchli ⟨Switzerland⟩ Chemists.

362 Herbert Auchli ⟨Switzerland⟩ *Galvanite.* Galvanisers.

363 John Alcorn ⟨USA⟩ *Dutton Co.* Book Publishers. Everyman Paperback Series.

364 Gerard Douwe ⟨Netherlands⟩ *Netherlands Railways Ltd.*

365 Erberto Carboni ⟨Italy⟩ *Toninelli.* Art gallery.

366 Magalhaes + Noronha + Pontual ⟨Brazil⟩ *Brazilian Institute of Geography and Statistics.* Graphic service.

367 Nedo Mien Ferrario ⟨Venezuela⟩ *Harry A. Jarvis.* Personal monogram.

144 368 Nedo Mien Ferrario ⟨Venezuela⟩ *Arthur Proudfit.* Personal monogram.

369 Max Huber / Studio Boggeri ⟨Italy⟩ *Scei.* Electric ovens manufacturer.

145 370 Erberto Carboni ⟨Italy⟩ *Radio Italiana.*

146 371 Walter Allner ⟨USA⟩ *Educational Broadcasting Corporation.*

372 Irving Harper / George Nelson & Co., Inc. ⟨USA⟩ *Howard Miller Clock Co.* Clock and lamp manufacturer.

147 373 Paul Rand ⟨USA⟩ *Consolidated Cigar Corporation.*

374 Allan R. Fleming ⟨Canada⟩ *Canadian National Railways.*

375 Lester Beall Inc. ⟨USA⟩ *Connecticut General Life Insurance Company.*

148 376 Ray Engle ⟨USA⟩ *Noland Paper Company, Inc.*

377 Everett S. Aison ⟨USA⟩ *Grossman Publishers, Inc.* Book publisher.

378 Neil Fujita ⟨USA⟩ *Sixth Inter-America Accounting Conference.*

149 379-380 Herbert Leupin ⟨Switzerland⟩ *Panteen.* Hair conditioner. (380 is used more frequently than the simplified version, 379)

150 381 Theo Dimson ⟨Canada⟩ *Julie's.* Restaurant.

151 382 Erberto Carboni ⟨Italy⟩ *Bertolli.* Olive oil manufacturer.

383 Marcel Jacno ⟨France⟩ *Gauloise.* Cigarettes.

384 Piero Fornasetti ⟨Italy⟩ *Corisia.* Fabric house.

152 385 Anton Stankowski ⟨Germany⟩ Holding company. (Project)

386 Vittorio Antinori Graphistudio ⟨Italy⟩ *La Caffetteria.* Coffee shop.

387 Yusaku Kamekura ⟨Japan⟩ *Bunken-shuppan.* Publisher.

388 Jaska Hänninen ⟨Finland⟩ *Boris Fehrmann.* Photographer.

389 Giancarlo Guerrini ⟨Italy⟩ *Alessio Bassi.* Cutlery manufacturer.

390 Heinz Waibl ⟨Italy⟩ *Radiotelevisione Italiana.* Quiz program symbol.

391 Jerry Braude ⟨USA⟩ *Nancy Lee Martin.* Public Relations.

392 Abram Games ⟨Great Britain⟩ *Inde Coope Ltd.* Brewer.

393 Walter Baumberger ⟨Switzerland⟩ *Comité International de la Croix-Rouge.*

394 Jerry Braude ⟨USA⟩ *Banner Printing Co.*

153 395 Christine & Ingo Friel ⟨Germany⟩ *Edeka.* Distillery of Gaston Cognac.

396 Christine & Ingo Friel ⟨Germany⟩ *Baade & Endrulat.* Container manufacturer.

153 397 Erich Buchegger <Austria> *Vollhumon.* Fertilizer.

398 Ernst Roch <Canada> *Marquesa.* Knitwear manufacturer.

399 Karl Oskar Blase <Germany> (Project)

400 Yoshiro Yamashita <Japan> *Yomiuri-shuppan.* Book publisher. Symbol for series.

401 Marco Del Corno <Italy> *Cave Carbonate Calcio.* Chemical manufacturer.

402 Lester Beall Inc. <USA> *The East Ohio Gas Co.*

403 Benno Wissing <Netherlands> *Amsterdam Commission for Publicity of Books.*

154 404 Herbert Leupin <Switzerland> *Schweizerische Käseunion.* Swiss cheese manufacturers trade union.

155 405 Push Pin Studios, Inc. <USA> *Automatique.* Food vending machines manufacturer.

406 Morton Goldsholl Design Associates. <USA> *Holiday Delight Co.* Bakers.

156 407 Yusaku Kamekura <Japan> Children's wear manufacturer. (Project)

408 Francesco Saroglia <Italy> *International Wool Secretariat.* Wool mark of quality.

157 409 Gerard Wernars <Netherlands> *Ten Cate.* Organization of textile industries.

410 Olle Eksell <Sweden> *Svenska Yllehuset.* Wool fabric industry.

411 Romulo Maccio <Argentina> *Aniversario Argentina.*

412 Olle Eksell <Sweden> *Melka AB.* Clothing manufacturer.

413 Romulo Maccio <Argentina> *Muestras S.A.*

158 414 Karl Erik Lindgren <Sweden> *Svenska Missionsforbundets Union.* Missionary union.

415 W. Hergoröther <Italy> *Zanichelli.* Machinery manufacturer.

416 Celestino Piatti <Switzerland> *Otto Butzberger.* Metal window frames manufacturer.

159 417 Willi Sutter <Switzerland> Knitted goods factory.

418 Gilles Robert <France> *L'Administration de la voie maritime du St. Laurent.*

160 419 Otl Aicher <Germany> *Schlaginstrumentfabrik Johannes Link.* Musical instruments manufacturer.

420 Ernst Roch <Canada> *Ross-Ellis Ltd.* Printer and lithographer.

161 421 Helmut Lortz <Germany> *Novum.* Graphic design group.

422 Kurt Wirth <Switzerland> *Swiss Travel Bureau.*

423 Karl Gerstner <Switzerland> *Schwitter AG.* Printing block manufacturer.

424 Gerd Leufert <Venezuela> *Institute of Industrial Design, Caracas.*

162 425 Takeshi Otaka ⟨Japan⟩ *Wagen-Shuzo Co., Ltd.* Brewers.

426 Allan Jungbeck ⟨Sweden⟩ *AB Kvarnmaskiner.* Grain equipment manufacturer.

427 Bertil Anderson-Bertilson ⟨Sweden⟩ (Project)

428 Walter Ballmer ⟨Italy⟩ *Confezioni Caliumi.* Dressmaker.

429 Carl Regehr ⟨USA⟩ *The International Telephone and Telegraph Corp.*

430 Gerd Leufert ⟨Venezuela⟩ *Control Center.* Industrial power supply.

163 431 June Fraser/Design Research Unit ⟨Great Britain⟩ *Slinger.* Commercial photographers, typesetters, and rubber stamp makers.

432 Frank Wagner ⟨USA⟩ *Nuhold American Corp.* Water repellent manufacturer.

433 Gerd Leufert ⟨Venezuela⟩ *Norte Sur.* Travel agency.

434 Walter Ballmer ⟨Italy⟩ *Laboratori Cosmochimici.* Chemical works.

435 Gerd Leufert ⟨Venezuela⟩ Artificial flower manufacturer. (Project)

436 Bertil Anderson-Bertilson ⟨Sweden⟩ *Boda Glasbruk.* Glass works.

437 Heinz Waibl ⟨Italy⟩ *Ceteco.* Carbon paper.

438 Romulo Maccio ⟨Argentina⟩ *Medium Publicidad.* Advertising agency.

439 Gerd Leufert ⟨Venezuela⟩ *Japanese Film Festival.*

440 Wim Crouwel ⟨Netherlands⟩ *Omniscreen.* Silkscreen printers.

164 441 Yusaku Kamekura ⟨Japan⟩ Japanese Association for the Promotion of Science. (Project)

442 Bertil Anderson-Bertilson ⟨Sweden⟩ *Svenska Stalpressnings AB.* Steel press. (Project)

443 Tetsuo Katayama ⟨Japan⟩ *Turner Color Works.* Art supplies manufacturer.

444 Yusaku Kamekura ⟨Japan⟩ Symbol for automobile. (Project)

445 Kurt Wirth ⟨Switzerland⟩ Electrical appliances manufacturer. (Project)

165 446 Jacques Richez ⟨Belgium⟩ *Conserveries Globus.* Fish canneries.

447 Yusaku Kamekura ⟨Japan⟩ Symbol for automobile. (Project)

448 Tetsuo Katayama ⟨Japan⟩ *Asada Iron Works Co., Ltd.*

449 Ove Engström ⟨Sweden⟩ *Svea Band & Pappers AB.* Paper and printing company.

450 Jacque Nathan-Garamond ⟨France⟩ *Herbst et Cie.* High-fidelity manufacturer.

451 Ernst Roch ⟨Canada⟩ *Dominion Oilcloth & Linoleum Co., Ltd.* Floorcovering and oilcloth manufacturer.

166 452 Toshihiro Kayatama ⟨Japan⟩ Pharmaceutical manufacturer. (Project)

166 453 Piero Sonsoni 〈Italy〉 *Sagdos.* Printer.

167 454-456 Toshihiro Kayatama 〈Japan〉 Pharmaceutical manufacturer. (Project)

457 Klaus Winterhäger 〈Germany〉 *Baumgarten Co.* Gas and water works.

458 Toshihiro Katayama 〈Japan〉 Pharmaceutical manufacturer. (Project)

459 Edger Kung 〈Switzerland〉 *Lucerne Boat Club.*

168 460 Walter Allner 〈USA〉 *Equitable Life Insurance Society of the United States.*

461 Herb Lubalin 〈USA〉 *Studebaker Co.* Symbol for the Lark automobile.

462 Giulio Confalonieri 〈Italy〉 *Gallery St. George.*

463 Max Bill 〈Switzerland〉 *Corso.* Restaurant.

464 Bradbury Thompson 〈USA〉 *Salomon Brothers & Hutzler.* Stock brokers.

169 465 Saul Bass 〈USA〉 *Panaview Sliding Aluminum Door Company.* Door manufacturer.

466 Antonio Boggeri / Studio Boggeri 〈Italy〉 *Eston Confezioni.* Men's clothing firm.

467 George Tscherny 〈USA〉 *Chairmasters.* Chair manufacturer.

468 Robert Sidney Dickens 〈USA〉 *Packaging Corporation of America.* Packaging products manufacturer.

469 Heinz Waibl 〈Italy〉 *Symphonie.* Foundation garments and bathing suit manufacturer.

170 470 Carlo Vivarelli 〈Switzerland〉 *Electrolux International.* Electrical appliance manufacturer.

171 471 Anton Stankowski 〈Germany〉 Constructors. (Project)

172 472 Neil Fujita 〈USA〉 *Pelican Films, Inc.* Motion picture producers.

173 473 Richard P. Lohse 〈Switzerland〉 *Escher Wyss.* Machine manufacturer.

174 474 Erberto Carboni 〈Italy〉 *Barilla.* Pasta manufacturer.

175 475 Kurt Schwarz 〈Austria〉 *Kurt Steinwendner.* Film producer.

176 476 Anton Stankowski 〈Germany〉 *Standard Electrik Lorenz Werke.* Electrical products manufacturer.

477 Ivan Chermayeff + Thomas Geismar 〈USA〉 *CIBA.* Information service of pharmaceutical company.

478 Erich Buchegger 〈Austria〉 *Austro-Chematon.* Scientific organization.

479 Anton Stankowski 〈Germany〉 Real estate agent. (Project)

177 480 Shigeo Fukuda 〈Japan〉 *Sankei Ad Monthly.* Sankei Press.

481 Max Huber 〈Italy〉 *Caprotti.* Cotton mill.

178 482 Max Huber 〈Italy〉 *Casino Taormina.* Restaurant and night club.

179 483 Frank Wagner 〈USA〉 (Project)

484 Yoshitaro Isaka + Keiko Takemura 〈Japan〉 *Toyo Rayon.* Product symbol.

485 Carl Brett 〈Canada〉 *Type House 1960.*

486 Elias Stieger 〈Germany〉 *Stieger Siebdruck Kaiserstuhl.* Printer.

487 M. Schneider / Studio Boggeri 〈Italy〉 *Studio per Industria Tessuti.* Textile studio.

488 Yusaku Kamekura 〈Japan〉 Mail order house. (Project)

489 Gerd Leufert 〈Venezuela〉 Lessons on Lithography by Leufert.

490 Yusaku Kamekura 〈Japan〉 *Taiyo Kikai-kogyo Co.* Machine manufacturer.

180 491 Tadashi Masuda 〈Japan〉 *Culleen.* Pencil manufacturer.

492 Takashi Kono 〈Japan〉 *Tokamachi Texile Association.*

493 Yusaku Kamekura 〈Japan〉 *Meguro Park Lane.* Bowling alley.

494 Gan Hosoya 〈Japan〉 *Asia Ski Manufacturing Company.* Ski manufacturer.

495 Luis Pals 〈Germany〉 Mail order house. (Project)

496 Giovanni Pintori 〈Italy〉 *Underwood.* Typewriter symbol.

497 Saul Bass 〈USA〉 *ALCOA.* Aluminum Company of America. Aluminum producer.

181 498 Bob Noorda 〈Italy〉 *Sonika.* Tape Recorder.

499 Kazumasa Nagai 〈Japan〉 *Kokusai Road Construction Corporation.*

500 Yusaku Kamekura 〈Japan〉 *Nihon Shinyaku.* Pharmaceutical manufacturer.

501 Takeshi Otaka 〈Japan〉 *Osaka Art Festival.*

502 Kenji Ito 〈Japan〉 *Canada Golf Shokai.* Golf goods manufacturer.

182 503 Koji Kato 〈Japan〉 *Sun Spice Inc.* Spices manufacturer.

504 Makoto Wada 〈Japan〉 *Light Publicity.* Design studio.

505 Kazumasa Nagai 〈Japan〉 *Nippon Research Center.* Market Research Company.

506 Gan Hosoya 〈Japan〉 *Kenchiku Mode Kenkyusho.* Architects.

507 Cecco Re 〈Italy〉 *Marketing Italia S.p.A.* Marketing office.

183 508 Kenji Ito 〈Japan〉 *Nippon Chromart Laboratory Inc.* Colour photography laboratory.

509 John Harrison 〈Great Britain〉 *Fisons Overseas Ltd.* Fertilizer and chemical manufacturer.

510 Leslie Smart + Sid Bersudsky 〈Canada〉 *Design Projects Center.*

183 511 Bob Noorda ⟨Italy⟩ *Metropolitana Milanese.* Milan underground railways.

512 Heinz Waibl ⟨Italy⟩ *Officine Calabrese.* Truck factory.

513 Jacques Nathan-Garamond ⟨France⟩ *Club Graphique.* Advertising Agency.

514 Giulio Confalonieri ⟨Italy⟩ *Ditta Piriv.*

184 515 Rene Weiss ⟨Germany⟩ Mail order house. (Project)

516 Shigeo Fukuda ⟨Japan⟩ *City Planning Promotion Movement.*

517 Tadashi Masuda ⟨Japan⟩ *Endo Kenchiku Sekkei Jimusho.* Architects.

518 Shigeo Fukuda ⟨Japan⟩ *Sanyo Electric Co., Ltd.*

519 Dieter Einickt ⟨Germany⟩ Mail order house. (Project)

185 520 Makoto Wada ⟨Japan⟩ *Toyo Rayon.* Symbol for product Pylen.

521 Otl Aicher ⟨Germany⟩ *Gral Glashuette.* Glasswares manufacturer.

522 Hiram Ash / George Nelson & Co., Inc. ⟨USA⟩ *Scott Paper Co.* Paper products manufacturer.

523 Unknown.

524 Roy W. Madison ⟨USA⟩ *Stanrey Corp.* Pressed metal equipment manufacturer.

186 525 Louis Danziger ⟨USA⟩ *Sun-dormer International.* Sleep trailer manufactuerer.

526 Nedo Mien Ferrario ⟨Venezuela⟩. *Lago Mar Beach.* Maracaibo nautical sports club.

527 Charles McMurray ⟨USA⟩ *Stephens-Biondi-Decicco.* Aadvertising arts studio.

528 Eranz Fässler ⟨Switzerland⟩ *Drawag.* Wire works.

529 Magalhaes + Noronha + Pontual ⟨Brazil⟩ *Editore Delta SA.* Publisher.

530 Bucher-Cremiéres ⟨France⟩ *Laboratoires Roland-Marie.*

531 Franciszek Winiarski ⟨Poland⟩ Trade Union of Building Workers.

532 Walter Ballmer ⟨Italy⟩ *Carema.* Wine.

533 Gerard Wernars ⟨Netherlands⟩ *de Swaan-Bonnist.* Trading company.

534 Nedo Mien Ferrario ⟨Venezuela⟩ *Ministerio de Agricultura y Cria.* Ministry of agriculture.

535 F.H.K. Henrion ⟨Great Britain⟩ *Rapp Metals, Ltd.* Steel stockist.

536 Joe Coroff / Promotion Design Associates ⟨USA⟩ *Film Projects Inc.* Film producers.

537 Helmut Kurtz ⟨Germany⟩ *Apotheke Ehrensperger.* Druggist.

187 538 Edward P. Diehl ⟨USA⟩ *National Society of Art Directors, USA.*

187 539 Joseph Binder ⟨Germany⟩ *Öffentliche Bausparkassen Deutschlands.* Association of home finance banks.

540 Walter M. Kersing ⟨Germany⟩ *Sitos-Werke.* Baking powder manufacturer.

541 Jacques Nathan-Garamond ⟨France⟩ *Tourist Office, Düsseldorf.*

542 Ernst Roch ⟨Canada⟩ *CIBA.* Pharmaceutical manufacturer.

543 Stig Lindberg ⟨Sweden⟩ *AB Gustavsberg Fabriker.* Chinaware, plastic and enamel goods manufacturer.

544 Magalhaes + Noronha + Pontual ⟨Brazil⟩ *National Touristic Service.*

545 Eduart Ege ⟨Germany⟩ Official emblem of Munich.

546 Marcel Jacno ⟨France⟩ *René Julliart.* Publisher.

547 Romulo Maccio ⟨Argentina⟩ *Sudamericana.* Publisher. Symbol of series *Coleccion Teatro.*

548 Anton Stankowski ⟨Germany⟩ Fodder manufacturer. (Project)

549 Roger Geiser ⟨Switzerland⟩ *Joseph Diemand.* Sanitation engineers.

550 Per Einar Egger ⟨Norway⟩ *Shoe Export Norway.* Shoe exporters.

188 551 Hisami Kunitake ⟨Japan⟩ *Seven Foods Co., Ltd.* Food producers.

552 Gustavo Balcells ⟨Argentina⟩ *La Mercantil Rosarina.* Insurance company.

553 Klaus Winterhäger ⟨Netherlands⟩ *Geldermann & Zone.* Dutch textile manufacturer.

554 Heinz Waibl ⟨Italy⟩ *Societa Generale Semiconduttori.* Transistor and electronic component manufacturer.

555 Heinz Waibl ⟨Italy⟩ *Societa Electronucleare Nazionale.* Electronuclear company.

556 Aldo Calabresi / Studio Boggeri ⟨Italy⟩ *Pirelli.* Electrical appliance and rubber goods manufacturer.

557 Vance Jonson ⟨USA⟩ *E.M. Miller.*

558 Frank Wagner ⟨USA⟩ *Warner Chilcott Pharmaceutical Co.* Products symbol.

189 559 Kurt Schwartz ⟨Austria⟩ *Magnum.* German magazine.

560 Paul Rand ⟨USA⟩ *Westinghouse.* Electric appliances manufacturer.

561 Paul Rand ⟨USA⟩ *IIT Research Institute.*

562 Masayoshi Nakajo ⟨Japan⟩ *Nido Industrial Design Office.*

190 563-564 Freeman Craw ⟨USA⟩ *Tri-Art Press, Inc.* Printer.

565-566 Giulio Confalonieri ⟨Italy⟩ *Ditta Boffi.* Kitchenware manufacturer.

567 Rolf Harder ⟨Canada⟩ Trucking transporters. (Project)

191 568 F.H.K. Henrion ⟨Great Britain⟩ *Cox of Watford, Ltd.* Steel furniture manufacturer. Ash tray.

191 569 F.H.K. Henrion <Great Britain> *Cox of Watford, Ltd.* Steel furniture manufacturer.

570 Theo Dimson <Canada> *Peterson Productions Ltd.* Motion picture producers.

571 Lars Bramberg <Sweden> *Nordiska Mässor.* Exhibition on roads and motoring.

192 572 Robert Pease <USA> *The Marin Jewish Community Center.*

193 573 Saul Bass <USA> "*Spartacus.*" Motion picture.

574 Saul Bass <USA> "*Man with the Golden Arm.*" Motion picture.

575 Saul Bass <USA> "*Advise and Consent.*" Motion picture.

194 576 Milner Gray / Design Research Unit <Great Britain> *Board of Trade Council of Industrial Design.* Rendering of Royal Coat of Arms.

577 Milner Gray / Design Research Unit <Great Britain> *Export Credits Guarantee Department.*

578 Milner Gray / Design Research Unit <Great Britain> *Ministry of Agriculture and Fisheries.*

579 Milner Gray / Design Research Unit <Great Britain> *P.&.O. Orient Lines.* Steamship company. Ship's badge for s.s. Oriana.

194 580-585 Milner Gray / Design Research Unit <Great Britain> *W. & A. Gilbey Ltd.* Distillers and wine shippers. Wyvern trademark.(various sizes and treatments to suit different puroposes)

195 586 Robert Perrit / Design Research Unit <Great Britain> *Westminster Wine Co.* Wine and spirit retailer.

587 Milner Gray / Design Research Unit <Great Britain> *Austin Reed Ltd.* Clothing manufacturer and retailer.

196 588 Hermann Eidenbenz <Germany> *Basel University.* Diploma and seal of doctorate.

589 Celestino Piatti <Switzerland> *Kinderhilfe.* Emblem for a fund providing school children with soap and milk.

590 Hermann Eidenbenz <Germany> *College of Music of Basel.*

197 591 Emil O. Biemann <USA> *United States Tobacco Co.* Symbol for Sano cigarettes.

198 592 Piero Fornasetti <Italy> *Rizzi.* Interiors and gift store.

593 Piero Fornasetti <Italy> *Ditta Fornasetti.* Mark or trays.

594 Piero Fornasetti <Italy> *Ditta Fornasetti.* Porcelain mark.

595 Piero Fornasetti <Italy> *Ditta Fornasetti.* Porcelain mark.

596 Piero Fornasetti <Italy> *Ditta Fornasetti.* Designer's mark.

597 Piero Fornasetti <Italy> *Ditta Fornasetti.* Porcelain mark.

598 Piero Fornasetti <Italy> *Ditta Fornasetti.* Porcelain mark.

599 Piero Fornasetti <Italy> *Ditta Fornasetti.* Designer's mark.

199 600 Piero Fornasetti ⟨Italy⟩ *Ditta Fornasetti.* Porcelain mark.

601 Piero Fornasetti ⟨Italy⟩ *Ditta Fornasetti.* Designer's mark.

602 Piero Fornasetti ⟨Italy⟩ *Ditta Fornasetti.* Porcelain mark.

603 Piero Fornasetti ⟨Italy⟩ *Ditta Fornasetti.* Porcelain mark.

604 Piero Fornasetti ⟨Italy⟩ *Ditta Fornasetti.* Porcelain mark.

605 Piero Fornasetti ⟨Italy⟩ *Ditta Fornasetti.* Porcelain mark.

606 Piero Fornasetti ⟨Italy⟩ *Ditta Fornasetti.* Porcelain mark.

607,608 Piero Foransetti ⟨Italy⟩ *Ditta Fornasetti.* Designer's marks.

200 609 Chwast + Glaser / Push Pin Studios, Inc. ⟨USA⟩ *Artone.* Artists' materials manufacturer. Studio India ink.

201 610 Verbena Rebora ⟨Italy⟩ *Ligure Lombarda.* Fruit preservers.

611 Morton Goldsholl Design Associates ⟨USA⟩ Meat packers. (Project)

612 Milner Gray ⟨Great Britain⟩ *Thomas de la Rue & Co., Ltd.* Banknote and security printer.

202 613 Fletcher + Forbes + Gill ⟨Great Britain⟩ *Goods & Chattels Ltd.* Fancy goods wholesalers.

203 614 Jane Sai ⟨USA⟩ *Hotel Sahara.*

204 615 Walter Allner ⟨USA⟩ *Reichhold Chemicals.* Chemical manufacturer.

205 616 Ernst Roch ⟨Canada⟩ Pulp and paper manufacturer. (Project)

617 Stephan Lion ⟨USA⟩ *Hoffman La Roche, Inc.* Pharmaceutical manufacturer. Symbol for Posidron cough formula.

618 C. Dradi ⟨Italy⟩ *Montecatini.* Chemical and mineral company.

619 Wojciech Zamecnik ⟨Poland⟩ Chemical products.

620 Kenji Ito ⟨Japan⟩ *Taiping Chemical Industry Ltd.* Chemical company.

621 Albe Steiner ⟨Italy⟩ (Project)

206 622 Ladislav Sutnar ⟨USA⟩ *Golden Griffin.* Book publisher; book retailer.

623 Nedo Mien Ferrario ⟨Venezuela⟩ *Cordon Bleu de Venezuela SA.* Food canners.

624 John Massey ⟨USA⟩ *Chicago Pharmaceutical Co.* Pharmaceutical company.

625 Giulio Confalonieri ⟨Italy⟩ *Galleria D'Arte Milano.* Art gallery.

626 Rene Althaus ⟨Switzerland⟩ Ex Libris.

627 Lane-Bender ⟨USA⟩ *Better Living Center, New York World's Fair '64-'65.*

628 Giulio Confalonieri ⟨Italy⟩ *Ditta Impermeabili San Giorgio.* Rainwear manufacturer.

206 629 Flectcher + Forbes + Gill ⟨Great Britain⟩ *Percy Haynes & Co., Ltd.* Paper dealer.

630 Peter Beck ⟨Germany⟩ *Arbeitsgemeinschaft zur Eingliederung Behindter in die Volkswirtschaft.*

Association to promote the employment of the handicapped.

207 631 Helmuth Kurtz ⟨Switzerland⟩ (Project)

632 Masayoshi Nakajo ⟨Japan⟩ *Kushihara Shokai Co.* Leather tanners.

633 Ernst Roch ⟨Canada⟩ *Carl A. Donald Excavation Corp.* Excavator.

634 Rose-Marie Joray ⟨Switzerland⟩ *Interessengemeinscheft Reinen.* Local planning association.

635 Christine & Ingo Friel ⟨Germany⟩ *Studio Friel.* Graphic designers. (own symbol)

636 Jun Tabohashi ⟨Japan⟩ Symbol for silk fair.

637 Rolf Lagerson + Stig Bark ⟨Sweden⟩ *Gense.* Stainless steel works.

638 V. Antinori ⟨Italy⟩ *Amore e Pollastrini.* Canner.

639 Elfriede Anderegg ⟨Switzerland⟩ *CIBA.* Pharmaceutical manufacturer.

208 640 Keiko Hirohashi ⟨Japan⟩ *Yaesu Piano Co.*

641 Tomoko Miho / George Nelson & Co., Inc. ⟨USA⟩ *Creative Playthings, Inc.* Toy manufacturer. Learning center division.

642 Keiko Hirohashi ⟨Japan⟩ *Tokyo Star Lane.* Bowling alley.

643 F.H.K. Henrion ⟨Great Britain⟩ *Penguin Books Ltd.* Book publisher.

Symbol for Peacock Books, childrens' paperback book division.

644 Martti A. Mykkänen ⟨Finland⟩ *Uusikuvalehti.* Pictorial magazine.

209 645 Celestino Piatti ⟨Switzerland⟩ *Scheweizerische Zahnarzte Gesellschaft.* Anniversary meeting of a national dentists' association.

210 646-676 The Organizing Committee for the Games of the XVIII Olympiad, Tokyo. Signs indicating various facilities.

Designers; Masaru Katsumi, Ikko Tanaka, Yoshiro Yamashita, Keiko Hirohashi, Tadahito Nadamoto, Akira Uno, Shigeo Fukuda, Wataru Ejima, Kuniomi Uematsu, Tadanori Yokoo, Tsunao Harada, Tsunehisa Kimura.

646 Official of the games.

647-652 (left to right): Woman Athlete, Man Athlete, Bath, Band, Shower, Post-Office.

653-658 (left to right): Lavatory, Club, Shopping Center, Sauna Bath, Ticket Office, Press Interview Room.

659-664 (left to right): Theater, Group Room, Dispensary, Clinic, Drinking Fountain, Dining Room.

665-670 (left to right): Telephone, Public Bus, Coat Room, Press Room, Lunch Room, Guest Room.

671-676 (left to right): Information, Locker Room, Bicycle Depot, Laundry, Olympic Village, Documentary Film.

212 677 Albe Steiner <Italy> *Teatro Popolare Italiano.*

678 Rolf Harder <Canada> Pharmaceuticals manufacturer. (Project)

679 Karl Erik Lindgren <Sweden> *Gumerssons Bokförlag.* Book publisher.

680 Hermann Virl <Germany> *Deutsche Bank.* Bank.

681 Magalhaes + Noronha + Pontual <Brazil> *Everon.* Photographic equipment manufacturer.

213 682 Anton Stankowsky <Geramny> *Friedrich Heyking.* Steel works.

683 Adolf Flückiger <Switzerland> *Tobacco Association of Switzerland.*

684 Armin Hofmann <Switzerland> *Pfauen.* Fasion center.

685 Rolf Harder <Canada> *Pharmacie Moderne.* Drug store chain.

686 Lester Beall, Inc. <USA> *Chance Vought Aircraft Inc.* Aircraft manufacturer.

214 687 Toshihiro Katayama <Japan> Pharmaceutical manufacturer. (Project)

215 688 Ikko Tanaka <Japan> *Kyodo Nyugyo Co.* Milk plant.

689 Klaus Winterhäger <Germany> *Firma Cürten.* Fishery.

216 690 Fletcher + Forbes + Gill <Great Britain> *International Scientific Systems.*

217 691 Morton Goldsholl Design Associates <USA> Electronics company. (Project)

692 Gerstner + Kuttner <Switzerland> *Swiss Watchmakers' Federation.*

693 Saul Bass <USA> *San Francisco International Film Festival.*

218 694 Franco Grignani <Italy> *Nereo Giroldi.* Reinforced concrete manufacturer.

695 Carlo Vivarelli <Italy> *Renggli.* Swiss interior decorators

696 Gerard Wernars <Netherlands> *Gevaert.* Film makers. Colored film symbol.

697 Morton Goldsholl Design Associates <USA> *Stone Container Corp.* Paperboard box manufacturer.

698 Olle Eksell <Sweden> *Landbrugets Avsaetningsudvalg.* Danish froozen food manufacturer.

219 699 Clifford Copeland <Canada> *The Canada Lithographing Co., Ltd.* Lithographer.

700 Fletcher + Forbes + Gill <Great Britain> *Anthony Blond.* Book publisher.

701 Kazumasa Nagai <Japan> *Nippon Design Center.*

702 Giulio Confalonieri <Italy> British-Italian import firm. (Project)

703 Armin Hofmann <Switzerland> *Mensch & Co.* Painters and plasterers.

220 704 Albe Steiner <Italy> *Pirelli.* Electrical appliances and rubber goods manufacturer.

221 705 Romek Marber 〈Switzerland〉 *Barnards.* Wire mesh manufacturer.

222 706 Fletcher + Forbes + Gill 〈Great Britain〉 *Designers & Art Directors Association.*

223 707 Chermayeff & Geismar Associates 〈USA〉 *United States Information Agency.* Symbol for exhibit "Graphic Arts U.S.A."

224 708-714 Competition of trademarks for *Electrolux International.*

708 Ernest Witzig 〈Switzerland〉

709 Ernest Witzig 〈Switzerland〉

710 Marcel Wyss 〈Switzerland〉

711 Hansruedi Widmer 〈Switzerland〉

712 Otto Krämer 〈Switzerland〉

713 Hansruedi Widmer 〈Switzerland〉

714 Hans Wydler 〈Switzerland〉

225 715-734 Yoshiro Yamashita 〈Japan〉 Symbols indicating various games of Olympiad, Tokyo.
(left to right): Track & Field, Rowing, Basketball, Boxing, Canoeing, Cycling, Fencing, Soccer, Gymnastics, Weight Lifting, Hockey, Judo, Wrestling, Swimming & Diving, Horsemanship, Shooting, Volleyball, Water Polo, Sailing.

226 735-736 Yusaku Kamekura 〈Japan〉 *Tokyo Olympiad.* Official symbol.

227 737 E. Mayerhofer 〈Italy〉 *Ombrasol.* Venetian blind manufacturer.

738 Harold F. Walter 〈USA〉 *Chicago National Life Insurance Company.*

228 739 Lippincott + Margulies 〈USA〉 *Olin Mathieson.* Chemical company.

740 Ivan Chermayeff + Gene Secander 〈USA〉 *Pepsi Cola.* Soft drink manufacturer.

741 Chermayeff & Geismar Associates 〈USA〉 *The Chase Manhattan Bank.* Bank.

229 742 Ettore Sottsass 〈Italy〉 *Olivetti.* Business machines manufacturer.
Symbol for Olivetti Elea 9003 Electronic computer.

230 743-744 Nelly Rudin 〈Switzerland〉 *Schwabenbräu A.G.* German brewer.

231 745 Gérard Ifert 〈France〉 *International Word & Picture Agency.*

746 Fletchar + Forbes + Gill 〈Great Britain〉 *George Hoy.* Typographic designer.

747 Ursula Hiestand 〈Switzerland〉 *Modissa AG.* Ladies' and childrens' wear manufacturer.

232 748 Siegfried Odermatt 〈Switzerland〉 *E.H. Schelling & Co.* Paperboard containers manufacturer.

749-750 Siegfried Odermatt 〈Switzerland〉 *Gottlieb Kistler & Söhne.* Sawmill.

233 751-752 Gerstner + Gredinger + Kutter ⟨Switzerland⟩ *Christian Holzäpfel KG.*

234 753 Herbert Matter ⟨USA⟩ *New Haven and Hartford Railroad Company.*

235 754-755 Otto H. Treumann ⟨USA⟩ *EL AL Israel Airlines.* Airline.

236 756 Yusaku Kamekura ⟨Japan⟩ *Tokyu Koku.* Tourist agency.

757 Otto Firle ⟨Germany⟩ *Lufthansa.* German airline. (Re-designed)

237 758 Michel Kin ⟨France⟩ *Mobilier International.* Homefurnishings.

759 Kohei Sugiura + Kiyoshi Awazu ⟨Japan⟩ *The Japan Council Against A & H Bombs.*

760 Kazumasa Nagai ⟨Japan⟩ *Suruga Bank.* Bank.

761 Thomas Laufer & Associates ⟨USA⟩ *San Francisco Seven.* Designer's group.

238 762 Tom Daly + Peter Max ⟨USA⟩ *Daly & Max Ltd.* Designer's own symbol.

763 Jerry Braude ⟨USA⟩ *Huntley Gaming Company.* Game table manufacturer.

INDEX OF DESIGNERS

Numbers refer to illustrations

INDEX OF CLIENTS

Numbers refer to illustrations